groundbreaking work that explains the inner workings of the game."
—*THE WALL STREET JOURNAL*

" Hollywood has needed one of these for a long time—a user's manual. This one could not be more complete. . . .[Grade] A."
—*ENTERTAINMENT WEEKLY*

" In his adroit charting of the confidence flow between the various entities and eras Mr. Epstein kicks up a lot of little surprises. . . Edward Jay Epstein is quite good."
— **LARRY McMURTRY,** *THE NEW YORK REVIEW OF BOOKS*

" . . . [A] valuable education for those seeking to enter and understand the entertainment industry. . . . Factually impressive."
—**JOEL HIRSCHHORN,** *VARIETY*

" Epstein peels away the Hollywood facade and gives a nuts-and bolts view of how the six entertainment empires—Viacom, Fox, NBC/Universal, Time Warner, Sony, and Disney—create and distribute intellectual property today. . . . [He] presents a fascinating look at the unbelievable efforts that must be coordinated to produce a film."
—*BOOKLIST*

" In vivid detail, he describes the current process of how a film is made, from the initial pitch to last-minute digital editing. There's a refreshing absence of moral grandstanding in Epstein's work. With no apparent ax to grind, he simply and comprehensively presents the industry as it is: the nuts and bolts, the perks and pitfalls and the staggering fortunes that some in the business walk away with. This is the new indispensable text for anyone interested in how Hollywood works."
—*PUBLISHERS WEEKLY*

" [A] meticulously reported new book."
—*THE BALTIMORE SUN*

" What one learns from these investigations is that the deepest, darkest secrets in Tinseltown have nothing to do with sex, drugs, blasphemy, or politics, and everything to do with money."
—*THE WEEKLY STANDARD*

" Edward Jay Epstein blew the lid off Hollywood's dirty little open secret."
—*THE WASHINGTON TIMES*

" Compelling. . . . [Epstein] demystifies the contemporary process of film-making in the digital age."
—*THE PITTSBURGH POST-GAZETTE*

ALSO BY EDWARD JAY EPSTEIN

Inquest: The Warren Commission and the Establishment of Truth

Counterplot: Garrison vs. the United States

News from Nowhere: Television and the News

Between Fact and Fiction: The Problem of Journalism

Agency of Fear: Opiates and Political Power in America

Cartel: A Novel

Legend: The Secret World of Lee Harvey Oswald

The Rise and Fall of Diamonds: The Shattering of a Brilliant Illusion

Who Owns the Corporation?: Management vs. Shareholders

Deception: The Invisible War Between the KGB and the CIA

The Annals of Unsolved Crime

Dossier: The Secret History of Armand Hammer

The Big Picture: Money and Power in Hollywood

How America Lost Its Secrets: Snowden, the Man and the Theft

Assume Nothing: Encounters with Assassins, Spies, Presidents, and Would-Be Masters of the Universe

THE
HOLLYWOOD ECONOMIST

THE FINAL EDITION

MONEY AND POWER IN THE AGE OF STREAMING

BY EDWARD JAY EPSTEIN

Parts of this book appeared in earlier form in *The New Yorker, Slate, The Wall Street Journal*, the *Financial Times, Gawker, Spy The Columbia Review of Journalism* and *TheWrap.*

For Susana Duncan

CONTENTS

PREFACE FOR THE 2024 EDITION

Death of a Business Model

_____

For most of 2023, the creative part of
Hollywood was paralyzed by a strikes the Writers
Guild of America, which represents most of the
writers of movies and television series, and a strike
of SAG-AFTRA, which represents most of the
actor and extras in Hollywood. Writers are the
creative element in filmed entertainment and actors
are the means by which it is realized. Without
them, the industry had little choice but grind to a
near halt between May and November. While the
double strike resulted in   adjustments to
compensation the use of AI, these changes

accomplished little more than would re-arranging the deck chairs on the S.S. Titanic before it sank. The sinking ship in the case of Hollywood was a business model that Hollywood had relied on for over a half century.

Prior to the advent of streaming, this business model had proved highly successful in keeping studios afloat. It was based on the idea that movies established intellectual properties for studios that could be exploited in many different ways over long periods of time. As Howard Stringer, then the head of Sony Pictures, explained to me in 1999 movies studios made their money not by the release of movies in theaters but by optimizing the licensing rights that they created on many different platforms, including broadcast television, video stores, cable TV, product licensing, and pay-per-view. To squeeze every penny out of each platforms, the studios' used time delays, called "windows," which specified the amount of time between the release of movies on each of these platforms. Through this system, money earned on these ancillary platforms, called in the trade the "back end," became the studios' principal source of profits from movies.

In addition, the studios also used their creative teams to produce series and other programming for television. This became an extremely lucrative sideline since they could later license these programs to foreign television. This television business, as a top Paramount executive told me could make "the difference between a profit and loss." Between their movie and TV business, the studios made money even as a theater audience defected to television.

This business model began to unravel in 2010 after telecom companies made the internet available to almost all the homes in America. These connections, backed by a government policy of "net neutrality" through which heavy usage of the Internet lines could not be penalized by the telecom carriers, made viable the business of streaming movies over the Internet. Netflix, the pioneer streamer, quickly demonstrated that people were willing to pay a monthly subscription fee to stream movies and television series at home or on their portable devices. Even more threatening to Hollywood, Netflix demonstrated thar it no longer needed Hollywood for its content. Nor did other streaming services. The proof was in the pudding. By 2024, Netflix had over 247.2 million paid subscriber, and it was rewarded by Wall Street with soaring stock prices and a market capitalization of $214 billion.

And Netflix was not alone. Google's YouTube, the leading streamer, had 2.7 billion monthly active users in 2023, which brought in more revenue than Netflix. Tik Tok, a relative upstart, which, like YouTube, streamed mainly user-produced content, had 1.2 billion monthly active users. By 2024, according to *Statista*, the worldwide steaming audience, was projected to produce 108 billion in revenue, far exceeding the revenue from movie theater audience.

The rise of social media competed with Hollywood for the global audience's attention as well as for its wallet. According to a report in the *Wall Street Journal* in September 2023, TikTok alone "now commands 95 minutes of user attention per day. Facebook and Instagram, which played 200 billion reels daily were rapidly catching up.

Some of the more prescient studio heads, seeing the handwriting on the walls, decided to opt out. For example, Jeffrey Bewkes, the chairman and CEO of Time Warner, foreseeing the coming transformation of the film industry, sold his company at the top of the market for $108.7 billion to the telecommunications giant ATT. Rupert Murdoch followed suit, selling his Fox studio to

Disney for $71.3 billion. And MGM sold itself to Amazon for $7 billion.

As the transformation unfolded, streaming services, with the exception of Netflix, began losing massive amounts of money ATT, and got out of the got out of the game by selling it studio to the Discovery Channel. A changing its name to Warner Bros. Discovery, it found the streaming business a hard nut to crack, and, in December 2024, it entered into talks with Paramount about the possibility of merger or takeover.

Meanwhile, almost all the remaining Hollywood studios, largely abandoning their previous back end based business model, plunged headlong into the uncharted business model of streaming. This required a massive reorganization of their legacy business. Disney launched Disney Plus and expanded streaming services. It also took fully control of Hulu, a streaming service with 48 million subscribers, by buying Comcast's one-third share December 2023 . Warner Bros. Discovery concentrated its resources on its new streaming service Max. NBC Universal, after buying Sky TV, launched the Peacock streaming channel. Paramount, after re-merging with CBS, launched its own streaming channel which included its

ShowTime channel, and called it, unimaginatively, Paramount Plus.

Hollywood's move into streaming was described by John Stankey, the ATT executive who oversaw the ATT takeover of Time Warner in 2019, as nothing less than a "paradigm shift." What partly drove this shift was the expectation that Wall Street would reward the studios with higher stock prices after they switched to streaming, as it had done for Netflix. To make this switch, they largely abandoned the system of time-delayed "windows." The move was largely facilitated by the closing of theaters during the Covid 19-pandemic in 2020. The immediate result, as an HBO executive explained to me, was that the studios "destroyed the platforms from which they made most of their money." The reality was that such ancillary markets as Video, DVD, TV syndication and foreign licensing had little role to play in the new streaming business model. The surprise part of the switch was that profits from subscriptions failed to make up for the loss of a large part of former back-end profits. The reds ink was beyond anyone's expectations. , "No one expected streaming to be this unprofitable," a studio executive told me. For example, Disney, had a cumulative loss of $11 billion from its streaming operation by 2024.

The problem is summed up by the geo-political joke "What are we fighting for, we all the same thing." The streamers were also fighting for the same audience/ There were simply too many streaming services wanting the same audience. Netflix, Amazon's Prime Video, Apples' Apple Plus, Disney's Disney Plus, Hulu and ESPN Plus, Warner Bros. Discovery's Max and Discovery Plus, NBC's Peacock, AMC's Sundance Plus, Paramount's Paramount Plus as well as smaller streamers such as Shudder, Acorn, BBC, PBS Masterpiece and Topic all wanted Since there are no impediments to entry, any content owner, no matter how small, can go into the streaming business from its own website.

But attracting subscribers in the streaming sweepstakes often requires creating or buying exclusive content. As a consequence of the competition for such content in the 2020s, the cost of making it rose astronomically. Warner Bros, for example, had to double its annual production budget from $4.5 billion to $9 billion in 2021 and Netflix upped its annual spending on new content to $17 billion annually, according to the *Wall Street Journal.*

Further compounding the problems for streaming-only services, such as Netflix, was that deep-pocked tech giants, such as Apple , Google, and Amazon, did not need to show a profit from their streaming services. For example, Amazon could spend spend a staggering $750 million to produce eight episodes of "Rings of Power," and

$11 billion for the rights to NFL football games for ten years, because, aside from paying the subscription fee, the prime audience it built could be expected to buy books, videos, music, medicine, groceries, and hundreds of other retail products through Amazon's prime service.

To get top original programs was costly. According to the *Wall street Journal*, Paramount, which was losing money at the rate of $2 billion a year on its Paramount Plus service, invested over $500 million in Taylor Sheridan's hit series "Yellowstone." and its prequels. Just one prequel, "1923," cost nearly $200 million for just eight-episodes.

The Achilles' Heel in the subscription model proceeds from the ease with which subscribers can cancel their subscriptions each month. Such cancellation churn rate. According to former Time Warner Chairman Jeffrey Bewkes, "a grievous error executives made in moving into the brave new world of streaming was not fully anticipating how high the churn rate could be." Since it is costless to cancel subscriptions, a subscriber does not have a compelling reason to continue paying a monthly fee once they have seen the movies and series that attracted them to a particular streamer. For example, many people who subscribed to Netflix to see Martin Scorsese's "The Irishman" in 2019, cancelled their subscription immediately afterwards. As a result, Netflix's $175 investment in this critically acclaimed film did not necessarily pay off in boosting longtime subscribers. Presumably, many subscribers take advantage of the cancelling option to see the fare on another service. According to *Antenna*, a subscriber-measurement firm, the churn rate doubled between 2020 and 2022. At last count in 2023, 25% of subscribers to Netflix, Apple, Disney Plus and other premium streaming services cancelled three or more of their services within two years.

In rethinking their business model, executives at Netflix, Disney Plus and other streamimg services struggled to find an alternative source of revenue. The answer they came up with, hardly novel, was advertising. After all, advertising had supported television for nearly a century. Why not add it to subscription streaming? An obvious problem here is that many subscribers had moved to streaming services to avoid interruptions by advertisers. So would they pay a fee to be bombarded by ads? On the other hand, ads could provide a more stable source of income than cancellable subscriptions. Streamers therefore decided it was worth a try. In late 2022, Netflix launched an ad-supported service in a dozen countries for $6.99 a month called "Basic with Ads," and Disney a followed suit with a similar ad-supported service for $7.99 a month. And by 2023, Amazon Prime had added layers of movies with ads called "FreeVee." But to keep advertisers' paying, the streamers, like broadcast television, had to guarantee advertisers a massive audiences. Finding such big numbers required programs that appealed to lowest-common denominator audiences. If streaming services adjusted their content to meet the requisites of advertisers, they might risk losing those subscribers who signed up for more elite and edgy fare.

Although streaming services with advertising eventually may prove profitable, the shift to it undercuts one of the Hollywood studios' little-known means of staying afloat—making and licensing series to broadcast TV and cable networks. Jeffrey Bewkes, the former chairman of Time Warner, pointed out to me that producing these TV series can be crucial to a studio's bottom line. The problem is that TV and cable networks are heavily dependent for their viewership on the cable bundles packaged by cable systems such as Comcast, Verizon, and Spectrum and the cord-cutting reduces this market. The more people who switch out of the cable bundle, the less money available to license the studios' TV products. Simply put, the switch to streaming undercuts, if not destroys, the studios' long-time golden geese.

As a result, cable, and broadcast TV fell below 50% of total TV viewing for the first time in history. It is hardly surprising that they now buy fewer series from the Hollywood studios. And without these TV sales, the studios find it progressively more difficult to make a profit.

For example, consider Disney. Its revenue from its traditional TV networks fell by 9.1% in 2023, operating profits from its cable assets were halved, and its operating margins reduced by 70%.

Compounding Hollywood's growing difficulties, the legacy business of making movies for multiplex theaters continued to wither away. That business depended on the studios' willingness to spend heavily on advertising new films in theaters. They could justify such expenses, at times more than $50 million for a single movie, because they could hope to make it back in ancillary markets. To this end, studios employed a system "windows," or delays, to optimize the revenue in subsequent markets, such as DVDs, Pay TV, premium cable, and TV syndication. But in 2020, in the midst of the pandemic, the windows system was effectively subverted by the the two largest movie studios, Disney and Warner Bros, who opened selected films simultaneously in theaters and on streaming. The ancillary markets were lost in the shuffle.

The collapse of the artificial spaces between different platforms meant that multiplex chains had to compete head on with streaming services for their dwindling audiences. Even though part of the theaters' audience was siphoned off, they still had to pay the same rent and other fixed overhead expenses. This added to the already precarious position of multiplexes. Cineplex PLC, the world's second-largest movie theater chain, filed for bankruptcy protection in a U.S. court on September 7, 2022. 2024 may be the year in . which the other multiplex chains join Cineplex PLC in bankruptcy court.

Multiplex chains, which book all studio movies, depend for their profitability, not on the success of any single movie, but on the total number of ticket buyers. Even with the success of such blockbuster movies in 2023 as *Barbie, Super Mario Bros. Movie,* and *Oppenheimer,* the theaters' total ticket sales in America were far lower than five years earlier. In 2018, they sold 1.3 billion tickets; in 2023, they sold only 878.6 million tickets. That might sound like a great number of tickets but before TV siphoned off most movie goers in the nineteen fifties, two billion tickets were sold in America in just 1949. Today theater chains like AMC have to contend with the reality that since 2018, movie-goers decreased by over one-third. For a theater owner such a decrease is a disaster. Fewer movie-goers not only mean fewer ticket sales but also lower popcorn and soda sales and lower on-screen advertising revenue.

No doubt Covid-19 helped diminish movie-going, especially during the lockdowns 2020-2022, but, whatever the cause, lower movie attendance leads to a doom cycle. Movie studios respond to smaller theatrical audiences by cutting the number of wide-opening movies they make for theatrical release. According to *Variety*, There were 88 films released in 2023 compared to 108 in 2019 Less wide-opening movies reduces the number of national advertising blitzes. Since these national ad campaigns drive audiences into theaters on weekends, they deprives theaters of weekend audiences, the lifeblood of their business.

Hollywood has always survived by having a viable business model. Its twentieth century model proved able to adapt to talkie movies, anti-trust suits, mandated divesture of theater chains, and the collapse of its star system. It survived such seismic challenges because of its lucrative back end. That back end dies with streaming.

Streaming services have a very different business model. Instead of a back end, they rely on monthly fees and now advertiser support. Whether or not Hollywood studios, with their huge marketing arms and overhead, will determine the future of Hollywood.

Edward Jay Epstein
January 1, 2024

INTRODUCTION

WHY WE DON'T UNDERSTAND HOLLYWOOD

There was a time, around the middle of the twentieth century, when the box office numbers that were reported in newspapers were relevant to the fortunes of Hollywood: studios owned the major theater chains and made virtually all their profits from their theater ticket sales. This was a time before television sets became ubiquitous in American homes, and before movies could be made digital for DVDs and downloads.

Today, Hollywood studios are in a very different business: creating rights that can be licensed, sold, and leveraged over different platforms, including television, DVD, and video games. Box office sales no longer play nearly as important a role. And yet newspapers, as if unable to comprehend the change, continue to breathlessly report these numbers every week, often on their front pages. With few exceptions, this anachronistic ritual is what passes for reporting on the business of Hollywood.

To begin with, these numbers are misleading when used to describe what a film or studio earns. At best, they represent gross income from theater chains' ticket sales. These chains eventually rebate about half of the ticket sales to a distributor, which also deducts its outlay for prints and advertising (P&A). In 2007, the most recent year for which the studios have released their budget figures, P&A averaged about $40 million per title—more than was typically received from American theaters for a film in that year. The distributor also deducts a distribution fee, usually between 15 and 33 percent of the total theater receipts. Therefore, no matter how well a movie appears to fare in the box office race reported by the media, it is usually in the red at that point.

So where does the money that sustains Hollywood come from? In 2007, the major studios had combined revenues of $42.3 billion, of which about one-tenth came from American theaters; the rest came from the so-called backend, which includes DVD sales, multi-picture output deals with foreign distributors, pay-tv, and network television licensing.

The only useful thing that the newspaper box office story really provides is bragging rights: Each week, the studio with the top movie can promote it as "Number 1 at the box office." Newspapers themselves are not uninterested parties in this hype: in 2008, studios spent an average of $3.7 million per title placing ads in newspapers. But the real problem with the number's ritual isn't that it is misleading, but that the focus on it distracts attention from the realities that are reshaping and transforming the movie business. Consider, for example, studio output deals. These arrangements, in which pay-tv, cable networks, and foreign distributors contractually agree to
buy an entire slate of future movies from a studio, form a crucial part of Hollywood's cash flow. Indeed, they pay the overhead that allows studios to stay in business. The unwinding of output deals, which started to occur much more frequently in

about 2004, can doom an entire studio, as happened in 2008 to New Line Cinema, even though it had produced such immense box office successes as the Lord of the Rings trilogy. Yet, despite their importance, output deals are seldom mentioned in the mainstream media. As result, a large part of Hollywood's amazing moneymaking machine remains nearly invisible to the public.

The problem here does not lie in a lack of diligence on the part of the journalists, it proceeds from the entertainment news cycle, which generally requires a story about Hollywood to be linked to an interesting current event within a finite time frame. The ideal example of such an event is the release of a new movie. For such a story, the only readily available data are the weekly box office estimates; these are conveniently reported on websites such as Hollywood.com and Box Office Mojo, which also attach authoritative-sounding demographics to the numbers. If an intrepid reporter decided to pursue a story about the actual profitability of a movie, he or she would need to learn how much the movie cost to make, how much was spent on P&A, the details of its distribution deal and its pre-sales deals abroad, and its real revenues from worldwide theatrical, DVD, television, and licensing income. Such information is far less easily accessible,

but it can be found in a film's distribution report. But this report is not sent out to participants until a year after the movie is released, so even if a reporter could obtain it, the newspaper's deadline would be long past. Hence the media's continued fixation on box office numbers, even if reporters are aware of their irrelevance in the digital age.

This book's purpose is to close gaps like these in the understanding of the economic realities behind the new Hollywood. In this pursuit, I benefited enormously from the help I received from people inside the industry. I was greatly aided by distribution reports, budgets, and other documents given to me by producers, directors, and other participants in the making and marketing of movies, and I am deeply indebted to several top studio executives who furnished me with the secret MPA All Media Revenue Report for 1998 through 2007 and with studio PowerPoint presentations concerning marketing costs. These documents revealed the global revenue streams of Hollywood films, including the money that flows in from theaters, DVDs, television licensing, and digital downloads.

I further thank everyone who answered my often-pesky e-mails (and my sometimes off-the-wall questions), including John Berendt, Jeffrey Bewkes, Laura Bickford, Robert Bookman, Anthony Bregman, Michael Eisner, Bruce Feirstein, Tara Grace, Billy Kimball, Thomas McGrath, Richard Myerson, Edward Pressman, Couper Samuelson, Stephen Schiff, Rob Stone, Michael Wolff and Dean Valentine.

I am grateful to Oliver Stone for casting me in a cameo part in his Wall Street 2: Money Never Sleeps in November 2009. This bit role allowed me to view the art of moviemaking—and it is an art as well as a business—from a perspective that I would not otherwise have had.

I also received an invaluable education in Hollywood law from Alan Rader and Kevin Vick at O'Melveny & Myers, which retained me as an expert witness in the Sahara lawsuit, and from Claude Serra of Weil, Gotshal, and Manges. These lawyers helped me understand the art of the deal.

I also am indebted to those editors who helped shape this material, including Tina Brown and Jeff Frank at The New Yorker; Jacob Weisberg and Michael Agger at Slate; Howard Dickman, Erich Eichman, and Ray Sokolov at The Wall Street Journal; Mario Platero at Il Sole 24 Ore; and Gwen Robinson at The Financial Times. Finally, I owe a great debt of gratitude to Kelly Burdick who suggested the idea for The Hollywood Economist—and brilliantly edited the book.

PROLOGUE

HOLLYWOOD: THE MOVIE

Hollywood has spent the last century making movies out of the great inspirational sagas of human history. Ironically, the one epic it has yet to make is one about a uniquely American achievement that has and continues to mesmerize the world: The Rise and Fall of Hollywood. Here is a true *Sturm und Drang* melodrama, full of fascinating characters from the edges who overcome seemingly impossible obstacles to build a new industry that today defines the world of mass entertainment. The scenario would follow the classic Hollywood three-act formula of Rise, Crisis and Resolution.

ACT ONE The Rise of the Studio System

Fade in on the men who founded the studios of Hollywood. These are self-made and self-educated Jewish immigrants from European ghettoes, who, before they got into the movie business, had been ragpickers, furriers, errand boys, butchers, and junk peddlers. They are true outliers: men like Louis B. Mayer, Samuel Goldwyn, Jack Warner, Adolph Zucker, William Fox,

Carl Laemmle, and Harry Cohn. To turn the magic of moving pictures into a viable business, they had to find a way of getting its movies before the eyes of enough viewers to repay them the cost of making the movies. After they first scraped together money to build arcades and nickelodeons to show movies, they moved onto to movie theaters which they owned and operated. To keep down the cost of making prints, they initially used bicyclists to deliver reels between their theaters. As movies become a national craze, they build distribution networks to service other exhibitors, and then studios to assure that they had enough movies. They didn't have to worry about audiences buying tickets, or spend large sums advertising, because in those days, there was no competition for their form of filmed entertainment. People just saw the posters outside the theaters, bought tickets for a dime and walked in.

Along the way, the new moviemakers had to battle part of the establishment in the form of the powerful Edison Trust, which, aside from its patents on electricity generation, holds numerous patents on movie cameras and projectors. When "the Trust," as it is ominously known, attempts to use the courts in New York and Massachusetts to take over the movie business, the movie-makers moved their studios to the newly incorporated village of Hollywood, a place they could control and build. By the mid-1920s, 57 million people—over half the American population—were going to their movies every week. Their theaters had grown into multi-thousand seat "palaces," as they called them. Their remarkable conquest of the American Dream, insightfully described in Neal Gabler's 1989 book, *An Empire of Their Own: How the Jews Invented Hollywood.*, is itself the kind of character-driven story that would become a staple of global entertainment.

Yet the saga is just beginning. These lowly-born immigrants, without any formal education, had to adapt to rapidly changing advances in information transmission   In 1927, less than a decade after they organized their studios, sound came to the movies. After audiences were mesmerized by Al Jolson in *The Jazz Singer*, these men, in one of the great technological feats of the twentieth century, converted most of the 21,000 movie theaters in America to sound and equipped their studios with sound stages. Their studios now needed stars with suitable voices for a national audience.   In what becomes known as the star system,   each studio created, and put under long-term contract, its own galaxy of stars for their talkie movies. By 1929, each of the major studio owned or controlled not only the stars and talent necessary to churn out movies on a weekly basis but the theaters to show them in.   Despite even the great depression of the 1930s, the weekly audience grew to 75 million, who go to their neighborhood theaters not just to see feature movies, but the studio's newsreels, comedy shorts, action-packed serials, and cartoons. A new generation of talent, including such brilliant innovators as Walt Disney, expanded its realm to children's entertainment, and another technological innovation, color added to the addictive power movies had on the public even in the bleak years of the Depression and the grim war years of the early 1940s.

Then the Second World War ended, the troops come home and by 1948, the studio system was at its zenith. More than 90 million Americans—two-thirds of the population—go to the movies on a weekly basis. The studios produced more than 500 feature movies per year, had all the major stars under ironclad contract, and employed more than 320,000 people. With the help of the government, their films dominated most of the global film market. Audiences in France, Germany, Italy saw mainly Hollywood's films. Their illusion-making technology was unmatched anywhere in the world. In little more than a generation, its founders have literally gone from rags to riches. The studio heads, now called "moguls" after Oriental potentates, are among the highest-paid executives in the world. But even beyond their movies, the Hollywood moguls were producing a less tangible form of wealth: the pictures by which the world at large defines the phenomenon of American culture.

ACT TWO   The Re-Invention

But two crises loomed on the horizon. The first proceeded from the long-simmering antitrust action, *U.S vs. Paramount.* A decision came in 1948 that effectively destroyed Hollywood's distribution system by severing the studios' hold on American theaters. In keeping with the consent decree they signed, they divested themselves of the theater chains they own and gave up their practice of forcing independently owned theaters to book an entire package of movies if they want any at all. As a result, they no longer controlled access to the theaters in which their movies were shown. For each of their movies, they had to negotiate with the new theater owners for opening dates and the division of the box office, which required small armies of lawyers, theater relations specialists and verifiers to check the ticket sales. With the loss of their control over theaters, the studios' star actors, at the behest of their newly empowered agents, refuse to sign new long-term contracts effectively ending the star system. The moguls now had to compete with independent and foreign producers for both theater bookings and stars.

The second crisis proceeded a new invention, affordable television in the late nineteen-forties. Even with its fuzzy black-and-white pictures, TV offers nearly free stay-at-home entertainment, which gradually captures a larger and larger portion of the studios' habitual audience. They now had to compete with home entertainment for their weekly audience. Whose ticket purchases in the early nineteen-fifties constituted almost their only source of revenue. They lost that battle when color TV was introduced in the mid-nineteen fifties. It was nothing short of disaster. The movies' weekly audience went into free fall and by 1958, it was less than half the size of the 1948 audience. Drive-ins, Cinemascope, 3-D, Surround Sound, and other innovations failed to get back the audience from television. The only way it could win back even part of its habitual weekly audience was to turn to its enemy television and spend small fortunes t advertising to create tailor-made audiences for each and every movie. The huge cost of this national TV campaigns often exceeded the cost of the movie, which was a prescription for financial ruin. The stock prices of studios plummeted to levels not seen since the Great Depression. Prophets of doom, seeing that entertainment landscape in America had changed to favor TV, predicted that the end of Hollywood was near.

However, the prophets have underestimated this generation of mogul's resourcefulness. For a half-century, its genius has been its ability to adapt to new circumstances. It is, after all, in the business of entertaining mass audiences, and those audiences, though diverted, have not vanished. So Hollywood reinvented itself. If the old studio system, with its contractual control of theaters and stars, was dead, the studios had a new system to replace it. Instead of just selling tickets, it would sell rights to its movies. After all, movies were a form of intellectual properties. it could exploit across any and all forms of entertainment around the world. In this new business model, it would use the theaters to showcase and pump excitement into the content, even if it they lost money. Its profits would come on other platforms. As Howard Stringer, then chairman of the Sony studio, told me "Our business is leveraging our content across multiple platforms. The studios collected "rentals," as they called their cut, from theaters, TV networks, home entertainment, video games, and toy merchandising.

In this new incarnation, Hollywood found new sources of revenue in licensing its movies to television, originating prime-time series, renting its movies on home video, putting them on planes and in hotels, reincarnating their characters as toys, and then, with the digital revolution, putting its movies on DVDs, Blu-ray discs, video-on-demand, cell phones, and the Internet. Since TV networks were then restricted by a Federal Communication Commission rule from having a financial interest in their programming, the studios become the main suppliers of prime-time television, which they could later sell to local TV stations in what was called "syndication". Even when the rule was eliminated in the 1990s, the studios kept their hand in the television till by buying television TV networks. It also greatly expands its reach overseas, creating yet another stream of revenue from syndicating the television series it produced abroad. This leveraging concept not only kept the movie business alive, it makes it central to the world's entertainment economy.

By the end of the millennium, Hollywood was no longer making a profit on domestic theatrical distribution or expected to. But the money flowed in from the so-called "back end." This included not only television, video, DVDs, pay-per-view, theme parks but foreign movie houses, video and DVD distributors and television networks. Indeed, Hollywood by now had become so dependent on these foreign markets that their demands for films ladened with spectacular CGI effects, continuous action and a minimum of nuanced dialogue became a crucial part of its green-lighting process for big budget films.

The profits from the back end were now so enormous that stars, writers, directors and producers demanded a cut of it, creating an industry for accountants, lawyers and agents. By 2009 the studios, which were never more profitable, had also changed. More of their employees were involved in marketing and distributing films than making them. The business of getting their movies to different platforms at optimal times had become far more complex. First, they made tens of thousands of celluloid prints of each major film, which UPS delivered through regional exchanges to as many as 16,000 theaters on a single day. Second, they poured tens of millions of dollars on TV and radio advertising to create potential movie goers to each of these theaters, as well as PR campaigns to hype them in magazine articles, newspaper reports and TV shows. Third, they made and marketed different versions for different countries, which required bonded agents to clear through customs, lawyers to negotiate compliance with local censors and bankers had to do complex currency conversions. Fourth, each film had a video and DVD version, which had to be manufactured, , stored in warehouses for months, and, about six months after a movie played in the theaters, the videos and DVDs of it were shipped to wholesalers, video stores and vending machine operators. Finally, as cable, pay-tv and TV windows opened around the world, which could be years later, still other versions of this film had to be distributed to this licensees. The mandated time gaps between the theatrical release and its release in video, DVD, cable, TV and others form were called "windows" and were considered crucial to keeping the movies theaters in business since anyone wanted to see a new movie had only one option: going to a theater. At each stage, of this convoluted distribution system, the studio got a cut called "rentals," and divided it with other participants in the back end.

All Hollywood sagas are supposed to have a happy ending, but not everyone in Hollywood was happy in 2009 because a new dark cloud was emerging on the horizon. It was the technology called streaming that allowed movies and television to be freely distributed over the global Internet.

ACT THREE The Streaming Tsunami

When Netflix first began streaming the studios'
movies in 2009, studios viewed it as another cash cow
they could milk. They figured Netflix, Amazon and
other streamers would need to license their premium
content to induce people to pay a monthly fee to
subscribe to their services. And they had hundreds of
thousands of hours of filmed entertainment in their
libraries, including movies, cartoons and TV series they
could license for a steep price, just as they licensed their
libraries for in-flight entertainment on planes.

For the first four years, Netflix, Amazon and other
streamers competed fiercely with one another to get this
content, and, in paying dearly for it, they provided a
windfall of billions of dollars into the studios' money
machines. What they didn't immediately see was that
the streamers had a brilliantly simple means to get
filmed entertainment before the eyes of viewers that
made the studios' convoluted distribution system look
like a Rube Goldberg cartoon. Instead of moving
physical replicas of their movies to theaters, warehouses,
wholesalers, video stores and other intermediary places
to great logistic expense, streamers would send it
directly to the TVs, computers of phones of a global
audience practically free. Instead of spending huge
sums in advertising to drive an audience to theaters and
video stores, streamers would have in place a
subscription audience that required no ad campaign to

mobilize. Instead of divvying up a back end to stars and other participants, the streamers, who had no DVD, video, tv or other ancillary platform, had no back end to split. The new technology replaced Hollywood's complex system. Streaming was hardly a new concept. As early as 1881, Théâtrophone began streaming Paris opera and theatre performances over telephone lines to those who subscribed to the service. In the early 1920s, George O. Squier, an American entrepreneur, patented the streaming system for transmitting continuous music over electrical lines that became the basis of Musak in stores and elevators. By, the turn of the millennium advances in computer power and data compression had advanced sufficiently so that both video and audio could be streamed over the Internet. This breakthrough allowed YouTube to be launched as a streaming platform in 2005. Netflix followed suit, and by 2009 it was streaming more movies than it was renting on DVDs. Amazon, who had all the servers and technology it needed in its cloud, followed Netflix into the streaming business, as did Hulu..

This existential threat that the century-old studios would be replaced by streaming became more apparent in 2013. Netflix, the leading streamer, announced that instead of licensing content from the studios, it would create its own original programming and own all the rights to it. This move not only would deny the studios the rich fees they were collecting from licensing, it would destroy their control over premium content. Netflix's first series *House of Cards* dispelled any lingering doubts that it could produce the premium content it needed. With this success, Netflix shattered the idea the Hollywood studios were necessary players in the vast new enterprise of delivering movies to a global home and mobile audience. Unlike previous technologies, streaming required no regional intermediaries to warehouse, store, distribute or license their product. It could be distributed directly to TV sets, Roku-type receivers, computers, tablets or mobile phone of couch potatoes and other consumers anywhere in the world. So Hollywood's production, distribution, the staggered "windows" from different platforms that had for nearly a century have movie theaters a monopoly on first-run movies, the PR machine , TV ads or a back-end were no longer needed. And as Netflix insisted on taking all rights on all platforms for everything they acquired, the studios would be denied the cut of TV, DVD, Cable or another ancillary platform on which they had relied on for most of their profits. Instead of employing vast cadres of PR and marketing specialists to create audiences, Netflix had a pre-packaged audience of subscribers who paid a monthly fee which constituted its entire source of revenue.

As other streamers, including Amazon, followed Netflix's lead, in producing their content, the Hollywood studios were left with a Hobson's choice. Either they could act as production companies for the streamers, as they had done for television networks for over a half century, or they could adopt the streaming model themselves.

Some of the more-forward looking moguls, seeing the handwriting on the wall, decided to cash in their chips and get out of filmed entertainment. Jeff Bewkes, one of the shrewdest studio heads in Hollywood, seeing the consequences of the streaming revolution, sold Time Warner, the studio he headed, for $108 billion to ATT. As Bewkes later explained to me. When ATT found that their aggregate earnings from their streaming business amounted to less than half of what it had been earning from HBO and other of the legacy network businesses, , ATT sold Time Warner to the Discovery channel. Meanwhile, Rupert Murdoch, the chairman of Twenty First Century Fox, sold the studio's Hollywood assets for $74 billion to Disney, which used them to build its own streaming service, Disney plus. And MGM, one of the oldest remaining studio, sold itself for $8.4 billion to Amazon which would incorporate them, including the James Bond 007 films, in its streaming service.

Their foreboding proved well-founded. Past great technological advances in the entertainment industry, including the movie soundtrack, home television, time-shifting video recorders, DVDs and Pay-per View, resulted in expanding the flow of revenue that went into the studios' money machine. Streaming was different. Streaming services had no interested in seeing their material on videos, DVD, pay channels or licensed to TV. They wanted it only on their subscription service.

Their business model therefore cleaved the single most important revenue streams from the studios.

As streamers became their own content-producers, they spent billions of dollars per month on creating their own filmed entertainment for their captive subscribers around the world. In a few short years, they, not the old Hollywood studios, wrote the biggest paychecks for production companies, independent producers, talent agencies, actors, writers and directors. Since their fare was intended for smaller screens than movie theaters, they did not need to achieve the Hollywood's high technical quality, and could produce filmed entertainment at $8 million per hour, which was a fraction of what studios spent for big movies.

The product that best fit their requisite of keeping subscribers paying their monthly fee was not Hollywood-style movies but series with multiple episodes that could go on for many seasons. Not matter how spectacular a movie was, a viewer, after seeing it, could cancel his or her subscription. A series could keep viewers subscribing for years. Series required show runners, who could keep the episodes flowing, while different directors could be hired for different episodes. Even more than they had been in televised soap operas, show runners became the key creative executives in the streaming universe.

By 2019, streaming services had all but taken over the global Internet. According to the 2019 Global Internet Phenomena Report video streaming, led by Netflix, accounted for 60 percent of all downstream traffic on the internet. One by one, the Hollywood studios joined Netflix, Amazon and Google's You Tube in the streaming revolution. Disney, aside from, Disney Plus controlled Hulu. Discovery, with the assets of

Time Warner, had Discovery Plus and HBO Max.
Comcast, which now owned Universal and NBC, had
three streaming services, Peacock, AMC+ and A&E, and
Paramount had Paramount+. Of the major studios, only
Sony had taken the option of producing content for
Netflix and other streaming service.

Studios could still make movies for at multiplexes
and no doubt youth still find them a place a good place
to congregate on weekends. But since the nineteen fifties
in has been a dwindling audience—only one-third as
many tickets were sold as in 2021 as a decade earlier,
partly due to the Covid 19-pandemic. But what made
their future even bleaker is that streaming services had
largely destroyed the window system that made theaters
the one and only place people went to see a new release
and made that experience an event. Now, with the
window system shattered, HBO Max and other streamers
released movies on their service while they were still in
the theaters.

But even if the studios through massive investments
in advertising induced the audience to return to movie
theaters, it would not solve the hole in their profitability.
In the platform business model, before streaming,
Hollywood studios could make huge outlays for TV ads
to establish movies in theaters because, once established,
they could make their profits in TV, DVD and the rest of
the back-end markets. But if streaming services
diminish these back-end markets, as seems inevitable,
the studios will wind up losing money on most of the
movies they release in theaters. In an age dominated by
streaming, their business plan based on profits from the
back-end rights no longer makes sense.

Streaming had also changed the relationship between
the consumer and the movie. "Whether it's a movie

ticket, DVD purchase or a download, the consumer was valuing a specific movie with a specific amount of money in the Hollywood model of distribution, "as Couper Samuelson, the President of Feature Films for Blumhouse Productions, pointed out to me. "But in the streaming era, the consumer is valuing a platform with an ongoing (monthly) amount of money. By definition, that reduces the "event" quality of a movie." In another words, movies, rather than being one-time events, were part of a large galaxy of filmed entertainment on a subscription service.

Hollywood changed to accommodate streaming services became the major creators of original content. Producers of films and series reoriented their companies to accommodate the shift to episodic fare, employing a new breed of highly-paid show runners and writers. Stars, who previously had been considered essential to create audiences especially abroad for individual films, lost the justification for 8-figure salaries. Streaming services did not need to pay Hollywood stars to garners a hundred million viewers for its series the Squid Game. It could gain such audiences at practically no cost, as Netflix did for The Squid Game, by using machine-learning AI to promote it to its own subscribers on the front page of its own service . Nor can stars, directors, writers and other participants demand a part of the back-end because, with the streamers buying all rights for their own service, there is no back end. In this new system, there is also no artful Hollywood accounting needed to divvy up so-called adjusted grosses, net break-evens or other payments tied to the back-end. Entertainment lawyers, forensic accountants, contract arbitrators and business managers, long the mainstay of the behind-the-scenes Hollywood business no longer had a back end to negotiate and enforces. This mean the nature of their work. Instead of working get stars a cut of future platforms, they now focused on getting them the most money possible from the streamers.

It also changed their relationship[with the movie theaters. When Hollywood began, movie theaters had been crucial to its economic success. Indeed, in its early years, it was its singular source of revenue. Culturally, they were the place where movie-goers, crowded together in a darkened auditorium to cheer, laugh, gasp, cringe and boo at what they saw on the screen, experienced movies. Even in 1929, the year that the Great Depression destroyed jobs and wrought untold misery on America, 95 million people a week, or 70 percent of the population, went every week to a theater.

Even when television another markets developed in the last half of the twentieth century, the theater launch in the United States. with its glitter, reviews and star appearances, remained such a crucial part of establishing its movies for these secondary markets that their contracts specified they have a prior release in American theaters.

This rationale for a theatrical opening all but ended when streaming took over the movie business. By

2020, it wasn't mere that the Covid-19 pandemic shut down movie houses but that the streaming of movies directly into homes ended the need for an expensive theatrical release. Business managers at studios asked top executives why spend upwards of $60 million to bring audiences into theaters if they could be more efficiently streamed to couch potatoes at home? All that was needed was for the studios to create their own streaming services/

By the end of 2020, all the major studios, with the exception of Sony Pictures, had created their own streaming services. The two largest movie studios, Disney (which had acquired the Fox studio) and Warner Bros. together accounted for over half of the nation's box-office. Both not only had their own streaming services but also released their movies on them simultaneously with their release at movie house. While Disney's service, Disney + charged for each movie, HBO Max gave all its movies free to its subscribers. As a result of these simultaneous releases, movie theaters no longer had an exclusive "window" on many major Hollywood movies. As a result, people had less incentive to go to a movie house. The results became evident at the box-office. In 2018, movie theaters had taken in $11.6 billion from ticket sales in the U.S. and Canada whereas in 2021, even after most of the theaters were re-opened they took in only $4.3 billion from ticket sales in the U.S. and Canada.

To be sure, the movie theaters still worked for w comic-book based blockbusters, such as Sony Pictures' billion-dollar hit *Spiderman: No Way Home/* The promise of mind-blowing special effects drew young audiences, mainly under 21, into the visual equivalent of an amusement park ride at the multiples and Imax theaters.

However, a large part of that audience was drawn away from other movies at the multiplexes. As the studios took a large cut of the box office from the Spiderman-type event movies, it depleted rather than increased the theaters' share of the box office. This meant the theater chains, which played all the movies in their complexes, profit margins were further squeezed. . For example, AMC Entertainment, the largest owner of multiplexes, which played *Spiderman: No Way Home* on large numbers of screens, lost nearly one-half billion dollars in 2021. Such losses, according to one knowledgeable former Paramount executive, signaled the beginning of a "death spiral" for the multiplexes. Nor was the trend friendly to movie houses. Between 2018 and 2022, they lost nearly two-thirds of their audience.

With major movie studios now engaged in the business of streaming competing movies to the home audience, the question became: how long could movie theaters survive? They had to rebate at least half their ticket sales to the studios—and even more in the case of big action movies such as *Spiderman: No Way Home*. And with the amount they retained, along with popcorn and soda sales, they had to the fixed costs, including rent, for each theater, multiplexes had operated on very thin margins even before the advent of streaming. By 2022, as major studios, including Disney, Warner Bros and Universal, who accounted for most of the movies played in the multiplexes, streamed movies that took movie goers away from their theaters, it added momentum to the death spiral. The smaller the potential audience for theaters, the less incentive studios have for spending huge sums for ads to make television audiences aware of newly-released films. According to Statista, their expenditures on TV ads fell more than 50 percent . between 2017 and 2022. The fewer the number of ads on TV, the smaller the audience for multiplexes every week. The smaller the audience, the less incentive the studios have to produce films for theatrical release. And so on.

The finale of the death spiral comes when the multiplexes chains wind up not taking in enough money from ticket sales and popcorn sales to their fixed costs, which includes pay rent, cleaning crews, projector bulbs and equipment maintenance. the suppliers and the employees and seek bankruptcy protection.

Can this death spiral be halted? Just as King Canute had no success in commanding the tide, the multiplex chains cannot command home viewers to come to the theaters or movie studios to make product for them

The sad reality is that as Hollywood moves further into the subscription system, it will have little, if any, need to create a separate audiences for movie theaters. Its objective has always been to get its movies before the eyes of as many viewers as possible at the least cost. Prior to the streaming revolution, it achieved this objective through a complex distribution system. First, studios would make tens of thousands of celluloid prints of each major film. Next, they would have UPS deliver them through regional exchanges to as many as 16,000 theaters across the country. Then it would buy 30-second ads on TV and radio that would typically be aired seven times during the week preceding openings to drive people to their local multiplex. They would then depend on these theaters to collect admissions and remit to them a share which has been negotiated by their legal staffs. For overseas distribution the studios had to make different versions for different countries, clear the prints through each country's customs and local censors and collect foreign currencies. And this was only for theatrical distribution. For video markets, studios had to manufacture edited DVD and VHS versions of each film, store them in secure warehouses and, when the video window opened, shipped to wholesalers, video stores and vending machine operators. Finally, they had to make other versions for the cable, Pay-Tv and TV markets around the world.

Hollywood executives put up with this Rube Goldberg-type distribution system, despite its inefficiencies, because they got a cut at every stage of the time-consuming process. That cut, called "rentals," was the main way studios made their profits.

Now that streaming provided a less convoluted and more profitable way of delivering their product an audience, studios had to consider vexing questions. Why split their films' revenues with the theaters when they can keep all the subscription revenue for themselves? Why employ armies of marketing executives, theater relations people and PR specialists to create audiences for separate movies, when they can let subscribers choose for themselves from a library of filmed entertainment   Why should they fight a more efficient and profitable business model in which their product can be directly delivered to consumers without going through theaters and other intermediaries?

The streaming revolution, like the adoption of synchronous sound in the twentieth century, is now an irreversible part of the movie business. Of course, some movie theaters will survive streaming, just as some vinyl records and 8-track cassette players survived the digital revolution. They can always find small niche audiences like the art houses did in the 1960s. But the principal business of the Hollywood studios will be producing content for their own subscription services. Their product will not stay the same. Its standard two-hour movie, which had such attributes of classical story-telling as a beginning, a middle and an end, rising and falling action, a climax followed by a denouement and happy ending—worked well to induce audiences to buy a ticket for a particular film at a movie house. It does not, however, fit as well into the business model for a streaming subscription service. The financial success of a streaming subscription service requires not that a person buy a single ticket to a single movie. If they joined for that purpose, they might cancel their subscription after seeing it.   Roughly half of U.S. viewers who signed up within three days of the release   such successful films such as Disney Plus's *Hamilton*, HBO MAX's *Wonder Woman 1984* and Apple TV Plus's

Greyhound cancelled their subscriptions their within six months, according the audience-measurement service Antenna.

The filmed entertainment format better-suited to keep subscribers from cancelling is multi-season series, like *Breaking Bad, Narcs* and *Squid Game.* In such format, as American soap operas and Latin American telenovelas have long demonstrated, audiences can be hooked for years by such devices as presenting new obstacles or opportunities for characters at the end of each episode. The success of this episodic format is easily measured, not by critical acclaim, but by how many eyeballs continue watching from episode to episode. And subscription services readily compile this data from their own computers. If the number is high, they can greenlight additional season or order other series with similar attributes. The result is that a well-tuned data-driven feedback loop largely replaces the creativity on which movie-makers had once prided themselves. In light of global money-making potential of the streaming model, a potential which Netflix and Disney have already demonstrated, the writing on the wall for the remaining hold-out in Hollywood is, in the words of The Borg on *Star Trek,* "Resistance is futile. You will be assimilated."

PAR T I

THE POPCORN ECONOMY

TWENTY-FIVE YEARS AGO, I LEARNED THE REAL SECRET IS THE SALT

Once upon a time, attending the local movie theater was an experience that most Americans shared on a regular basis. For example, in 1929, the year of the first Academy Awards, an average of ninety-five million people—about four-fifths of the ambulatory population—went to movies every week. There were more than twenty-three thousand theaters, many of palatial size, like the six-thousand two-hundred-seat Roxy in New York. In those days, the major studios made virtually all the movies that people saw (over seven hundred feature films in 1929). The stars, directors, writers, and other talent were under exclusive contract, and, in addition, the studios owned the theatrical circuits where first-run movies played. This regime, which allowed the major studios to exert total control over movies, from script to screen, came to be known, and feared, as "the studio system"; it more or less ended in 1950, when the United States Supreme Court upheld antitrust decrees ordering several of the major Hollywood studios to divest themselves of their theater chains.

Today, in a world with television, video, the Internet, and other home diversions, weekly average movie attendance is about thirty million, or less than 10 percent of the population. As a result of this diminishment, many larger theaters either closed or divided themselves into smaller auditoriums under one roof. (There are only a third as many theater sites today as there were in 1929, but there are more screens—over thirty thousand.) These multiplexes afforded theater owners significant economies of scale. They could also show a greater variety of films, tailored to different, if smaller, audiences. And as smaller theaters closed the chains expanded; today, the fifteen largest North American chains own approximately two-thirds of all the screens. These large chains, and their centralized film bookers, are the principal gatekeepers for the American film industry. They are responsible for determining what movies most Americans see.

Today a handful of nation-wide multiplex chains account for more than 80 percent of Hollywood's share of the American box office, and a large share of these bookings are done at ShoWest, the annual event in Las Vegas in which movie distribution and exhibition executives meet over four days to discuss plans for releasing and marketing upcoming films. In 1998, I contacted Thomas W. Stephenson, Jr., who then headed one of these major chains, Hollywood Theaters, and arranged to accompany him to ShoWest. Stephenson was willing to let me tag along to meetings in Las Vegas on the condition that I not directly quote or identify those with whom he met. As part of the deal, he agreed to a Don't Ask, Don't Tell protocol in which, unless they specifically asked, he would not identify me as a journalist to the other participants at these meetings with bankers and studio executives.

On the way to Las Vegas, Stephenson, an energetic, peppery-haired man in his early forties, gave me a quick course in the economics of his business. Of the $50 million customers that paid for tickets in 1997, he said his 450-screen chain, Hollywood Theaters, kept only $23 million; most of the rest went to the distributors. But, he continued, since it cost $31.2 million to pay the operating costs of the theaters, his company would have lost $8.2 million if it were limited to the movie-exhibition business. Like all theater owners, though, he has a second business: snack foods, in which the profit margin is well over 80 percent. And with the snack foods, Hollywood Theaters made a profit of $22.4 million on the sale of $26.7 million from its concession stands. "Every element in the lobby," Stephenson told me, "is designed to focus the attention of the customer on its menu boards."

When we arrived, he decided to skip the reception hosted by independent distributors. "I personally enjoy watching many of the low-budget films that come from independents," he said, "but they are not a significant part of our business." In fact, according to Stephenson, 98 percent of the admission revenues of his theater in 1997 came from the principal Hollywood studios—Sony, Disney, Fox, Universal, Paramount, and Warner Bros. These companies supplied his multiplexes not only with films but with the essential marketing campaigns that accompany them. (Occasionally, to be sure, independent films do succeed in winning a mass audience, as, for example, *The Full Monty* and *Slumdog Millionaire* did; but, as Stephenson put it, "We don't count on them.")

Marketing campaigns begin months before the release date, use the most sophisticated methods available to target demographic groups, and intensify their activity in the final week, often with saturation television advertising, in order to capture "impulse" moviegoers. Stephenson and other theater owners rely on them to muster, if not to create, the audience for a film's crucial opening weekend. The campaigns require massive resources. The major studios spent, on average, $19.2 million in 1997 to advertise each of their films, a sum that would be considerably higher if it included the advertising provided by fast-food restaurants, toy companies, and other retailers in promotional tie-in arrangements that can amount to many times what the studio itself budgets. Rather than attend the large reception, therefore, on our first night we dined with the representative of Coca-Cola, a company that exclusively "pours" the soft drinks in over 70 percent of American movie theaters, including Stephenson's. Soft drinks are an important part of the movie business. All the seats in Stephenson's new theater, and most other multiplexes, are now equipped with their own cup holders, a feature that theater executives consider one of the most groundbreaking innovations in movie-theater history. With cup holders, customers can not only handle drinks more easily in combination with other snacks but can store their drinks while returning to the concession stand for more food. Hollywood Theaters, which now offers an oversized plastic cup with unlimited refills, sold slightly in excess of $11 million dollars-worth of Coca-Cola products in 1997, of which well over $8 million was profit.

Although most of ShoWest's official functions take place in convention halls and hospitality suites at Bally's Hotel, much unofficial business was done in its sprawling coffee shop. It was there early the next morning that I joined Stephenson for a breakfast meeting with an analyst from J. C. Bradford & Co., an investment firm. Acquisitions were in the air; Kohlberg Kravis Roberts had just bought and consolidated two of the largest theater chains. Stephenson, as he made clear at the outset, planned to partake in this industry consolidation by acquiring state of-the-art multiplexes. Since he planned to finance this aggressive expansion by selling part of his company to public or private investors, he needed the services of investment bankers who, in turn, needed a story or convincing rationale, to raise the money.

Stephenson's story centered on stadium seating, in which every row of seats is elevated about fourteen inches above the row preceding it, allowing all customers to have an unimpeded view of the screen. While the seats take up more space, Stephenson said, "Our focus groups show that people now seek out theaters with stadium seating and will drive as far as twenty miles to find one that has it." Attendance increased between 30 and 52 percent where he had installed such seating. Stephenson would repeat this story to four other investment bankers at similar kaffeeklatsches over the next two days.

A little later, Stephenson moved to a different table to meet with two of the top executives of another major chain. He had told me beforehand that he wanted to buy five of their multiplexes and sell them an equivalent number in different locations, or "zones." In the movie business, the country is divided into zones that contain anywhere from a few thousand to a few hundred thousand people; the major distributors license their films to only one theater owner in each zone. Just over two-thirds of Stephenson's theaters are in such exclusive zones, and he wanted to increase this number. These talks ended inconclusively, and in the late morning I accompanied Stephenson to the convention hall, where we took assigned seats in the grandstands. Stephenson, along with 3,600 other attendees, was there to see the first major studio presentation, Sony's product reel. Sony's top executives sat on a dais, as if addressing a shareholders' meeting. Jeff Blake, the president of Sony's distribution arm, said that last year Sony films had brought a new record gross into American theaters: $1.2 billion. Indeed, Sony accounted for nearly one out of every four dollars spent on movie tickets in 1997.

Vanna White, the television personality, then conducted a mock *Wheel of Fortune* game in which every clue referred to films coming from Sony in the next year, including *Godzilla*. As Vanna White announced each title, actors from the film in question rushed onto the stage—among them such stars as Michelle Pfeiffer, Julia Roberts, Nicolas Cage, and Antonio Banderas. All of this was followed by excerpts from the films. A highlight of sorts came when the stage suddenly filled with dancers costumed as characters from Sony's movies. Robert Goulet played the part of Jeff Blake and sang, to the tune of "The Impossible Dream":

*This is our quest, to be king of the box
There'll be lines round the block
When that big hunk Godzilla is finally
here And you'll know what we've done*

for you lately When we beat the
unbeatable year.

A private meeting held afterward, in Sony's Las
Vegas conference room, was far more grounded in
reality. A top Sony executive immediately set the
tone by observing that the presentation had cost
Sony four million dollars (a gross exaggeration, it
turned out) and then quipped that next year, instead
of hosting the event, Sony would just send a ten-
thousand-dollar check to each of the chains' film
buyers. It became apparent at this meeting that the
negotiations did not concern whether a chain would
show Sony films on their prescribed release dates;
that was taken for granted. At issue was the terms
under which they were to be played and positioned
against the films of competing distributors, for
instance, the number of screens they would be
shown on in a multiplex, the guaranteed length of
each film's run, the amount of free advertising there
would be in the form of trailers and lobby displays,
and the division of the box office receipts.

For example, regarding *Godzilla*, the executive
outlined the enormous marketing campaign,
supported by worldwide licensees of three thousand
Godzilla products, as well as promotional tie-ins
with such retail partners as Taco Bell, Sprint,
Swatch, Hershey's, Duracell, Kirin beer, and
Kodak, which were designed to drive a huge and
voracious audience of teen-age boys to their

theaters. This particular audience, as he described it, was not concerned with the quality of the film, or even whether it was in focus, as long as there was action and popcorn. He joked that the theaters' potential popcorn sales should persuade them to agree to give Sony a larger opening week cut. Joke or not, the implication was not lost on Stephenson's film buyer, although for the moment he successfully resisted Sony's suggestion. (As it turned out, the *Godzilla* campaign succeeded in "driving" people to pay seventy-four million dollars to see the poorly reviewed lizard in its opening, Memorial Day weekend.)

The next private meeting, in the hospitality suite of Twentieth Century Fox, was more relaxed. After offering Stephenson a soft drink, the Fox executive discussed the strategy for the summer season, which provides the largest audience for theaters. Indeed, of the nearly 1.4 billion tickets sold in 1997, some five hundred million were for the summer season, when, as the Fox executive put it, "Every day is a school holiday." (Another two hundred and thirty million were sold in the so-called holiday season, between Thanksgiving and New Year's.)

For the summer release season, Fox was facing competition from a number of catastrophe films, such as *Godzilla, Deep Impact*, and *Armageddon*, which early tracking polls showed were attracting the attention of large numbers of male teens. The polls I saw, which were conducted by the National Research Group, had divided respondents into five demographic "quadrants"—under twenty-five, over twenty-five, male, female, and a racial category—and asked about their awareness of, and interest in, upcoming films. On the basis of these data, along with other research supplied by the company, the major studios can avoid simultaneously competing in the same demographic categories and dividing up their opening-weekend audiences. Even in March, the Fox executive reckoned that competitors' films, particularly *Godzilla* and *Armageddon*, would dominate two crucial quadrants—male and under twenty-five—in the early summer. He therefore opted to counter-program, which meant scheduling romantic comedies, that would appeal to the female and over-twenty-five quadrants.

Although the Fox people had an easier style than their Sony counterparts, they wanted the same limited commodity: the chain's better screens, play dates, and in-theater advertising. So did the four other distributors Stephenson met with during ShoWest. By his count, in four days he watched brief excerpts from some fifty films. "They all tend to blur together," he said, and plots were never described. Instead, the accompanying pitches identified them in such jargon as "Clearasil" (coming of-age), "genre" (teen-age horror), "romantic comedy" (love story), "ethnic" (black characters), "franchise" (the carbon-copy sequel of another film), and "catastrophe" (volcano, comet/asteroid/monster, loud sound effects). The Holy Grail was a film like *Titanic*, which appealed to all five quadrants. The last and longest meeting was with Disney's distribution arm, Buena Vista; its senior executives were eager to spend an hour or so discussing marketing plans with Stephenson. While they voiced some concern about the proximity of July's *Armageddon*, in which the earth is on a fatal collision path with an asteroid, with Paramount and DreamWorks' *Deep Impact*, in which the world is on a fatal collision path with a comet, they had an ingenious scheme for differentiating their product. Holding up a rectangular box, their executives explained that it contained a kit that would help theater managers to build a mock asteroid. Disney planned to distribute this package to theaters playing *Armageddon* and award prizes to theater managers who used it to create the most forbidding cosmic rock. The theme would then be amplified through such stunts as end-of-the world parties hosted by local disc jockeys.

Later, Stephenson, along with several of his top executives, toured the trade-show pavilions located in two giant tents behind Bally's, where delegates to ShoWest were somewhat greedily sampling popcorn, jellybeans, chocolates, licorice, frankfurters, nachos, and other snacks, many of which claimed innovative new flavors and aromas.

Others were getting a look at the non-consumable products at the booths, such as loudspeakers, projectors, ticket rolls, cleaning equipment, marquee letters, plastic cups, and remote ticketing systems. As we walked around, one of Stephenson's associates stopped to try an oversized Wetzel's pretzel. According to the pretzel company's representative, the Wetzel's, though about three hundred calories, would appeal to diet-conscious non-popcorn-eaters, such as women who wait on the concession line with their boyfriends. At this point, one of Stephenson's top executives, who was assessing different popcorn-topping oil, said to me in a hushed tone that "The real secret is the salt." As a veteran of the movie exhibition business, he explained that the more salt that a movie theater added to the butter it poured over its popcorn, the more money it made since it drove customers back to the concession stand for drinks—where they buy more popcorn. Stephenson concurred, adding, "We are in a very high-margin retail business."

WHY DO MOST NEW MOVIE THEATERS HAVE FEWER THAN 300 SEATS?

The multiplex can be traced back to an otherwise unmemorable shopping center in Kansas City, Missouri in 1963. Its theater owner Stanley H. Durwood split one theater into two "screens," allowing a single box office and concession stand to service audiences watching two different films. In addition, new automated projectors allowed a single untrained (and non-union) projectionist to run an entire program, including trailers, advertisements, and the movie for multiple screens. The arrangement proved so profitable that Durwood's company, American Multi-Cinema, or AMC as it is now known, along with the other major chains, converted most, indeed almost all, of the large movie palaces in America into multiplexes.

What greatly contributed to the shrinking of the multiplex auditoria, or "screens," was the Americans with Disabilities Act (ADA) of 1990. This act requires that new or renovated public theaters with more than 299 seats provide wheelchair access to all rows. Providing such access requires up to one-third more space for the necessary ramps—space that cannot be filled with revenue generating seats. To avoid this problem, multiplex owners divided their space into smaller theaters with a maximum of 299 seats. The result was a further proliferation of screens. Between 1990 and 2005 the total number of screens in the United States rose from 23,000 to nearly 38,000. Since multiplex owners essentially are in the people moving business—moving as many people as possible per hour past their concession stands—they found that the best way to maximize this "flow," as one multiplex owner explained, was to show the movies expected to draw the largest audiences on different screens every hour or even half-hour. So the same movies were booked on multiple screens at a single multiplex.

This strategy has recently undermined the studio's system of "zones" and "clearances" in which the studio's distribution arms refuse to provide the same movie to competing theaters in the same locale. This practice made sense in the era of neighborhood movie theaters. Theater owners insisted they needed such protection to prevent audience confusion proceeding from people seeing the same movie playing at two nearby theaters. And studios accommodated even though it meant that they had to have a larger inventory of movies available to make allocations to a larger number of theaters.

This restrictive system became unnecessary when multiplex owners moved towards smaller theaters to deal with the ADA. What multiplexes now wanted were the most heavily advertised new blockbusters even if they were playing across the street (or mall). As Richard Myerson, the general manager of Twentieth Century Fox's distribution arm explained to me, "multiplexes were no longer competing with one another for different movies." They simply wanted to attract a bigger flow of popcorn eaters to their entertainment complex. So as theaters no longer wanted it, the studios happily ended the system.

The consequence of this chain of events is that studios found themselves needing to distribute fewer movies. And this allowed them to further concentrate their resources on producing the action-packed franchise movies that help multiplexes maintain their flow of teen foot traffic past concession stands. Instead of a diverse portfolio of movies, studios could now open a franchise movie such as *Batman Begins, Transformers 2*, or *Spider-Man 3* on 4,000 or more screens and, if successful, get huge grosses flowing through the box offices.

The only downside for studios is that opening on more, smaller screens requires more prints. Back in the 1970s a studio could open a movie with 800 prints (an outlay of $800,000)—even *Star Wars*, the biggest hit of its time, never played on more than 1,100 screens. But with wider openings the cost of prints became far more substantial. With each print costing about $1,500, opening on 4,000 screens requires an outlay of $6 million.

The butterfly effect may even tip the scales in favor of digital projection in the coming decade. After all, if smaller screens continue to replace larger ones because of the ADA challenge, the simplest way that studios have to offset the growing print and distribution cost is to help subsidize a shift in multiplexes from analog to digital projectors. The advantage to studios, as one Paramount executive suggested, is that a studio could open a movie in "30,000 theaters around the world, if only for a weekend," and capture the huge cash-flow that would come from a global campaign. Such a vision, alas, might not bode well for those who enjoy less-action packed non-blockbusters.

SEX IN THE CINEMA:
ASSET OR LIABILITY?

In the early days of Hollywood, nudity—or the illusion of it—was considered such an asset that director Cecil B. DeMille famously made bathing scenes an obligatory ingredient of his biblical epics. Nowadays, nudity may be a decided liability when it comes to the commercial success of a movie. The top twenty-five grossing films since 2000— including such franchises as *Spider-Man, Lord of The Rings, Shrek, Harry Potter, Batman*, and *The Incredibles*, contained no sexually oriented nudity. In fact, the absence of sex—at least graphic sex—is often key to the success of Hollywood's moneymaking movies since it increases the potential audience of children in both the domestic and foreign markets. To be sure, directors may consider a sex scene artistically integral to their movie, but studios almost always have the right to exercise the final cut, and, if they want to maximize the potential revenue, they have to consider three factors.

First, there is the rating system. For a film to play in movie theaters belonging to the National Association of Theater Owners—which includes all the multiplexes in America—it first needs to obtain a rating from a board organized by the Motion Picture Association of America, the trade association of the six major studios. All the expenses for rating movies are paid to the MPAA by the studio out of a percentage deducted from box office receipts. As it presently works, a movie that contains sexually oriented nudity gets either an NC-17 or an R rating, depending on how graphically sex is depicted. The NC-17 rating, which forbids theaters from admitting children under the age of eighteen, is the equivalent of a death sentence as far as the studios are concerned. In fact, since the financial disaster of Paul Verhoeven's NC-17 *Showgirls* in 1995, no studio has attempted a wide release of a NC-17 film. As one Paramount executive suggested, because of their sexually related nudity, movies such as Louis Malle's *Pretty Baby*, Bernardo Bertolucci's *Last Tango in Paris*, and Stanley Kubrick's *A Clockwork Orange* would not even be considered by a major studio today.

If a movie contains less explicit nudity, it earns an R rating, which merely prohibits youth unaccompanied by an adult. Even though this option means that some number of multiplex employees—who might otherwise be selling popcorn—are required to check the identity documents of the teenage audience, theaters accept R-rated films, as was the case with *Troy*, if the R is for graphic violence because movie violence is a huge attraction for the teen audience. An R rating for nudity has a further problem in the popcorn economy: it greatly complicates the movie's all-important marketing drive. When a film receives an R rating for nudity, many television stations and cable networks, particularly teenage-oriented ones, will not accept TV ads for the movie. In addition, an R rating for nudity will preclude any of the fast-food chains, beverage companies, or toy manufacturers that act as the studios' merchandise tie-in partners from backing the movie with tens of millions of dollars in free advertising. As a result, it becomes much more expensive to alert and herd audiences to theaters for R-rated films.

Second, there is the Wal-Mart consideration. In 2007, the six studios took in $17.9 billion from DVD sales, according to the studios' own internal numbers. Wal-Mart, including its Sam's Club stores, accounted for nearly one quarter of those sales, which means that Wal-Mart wrote more than $4 billion in checks to the studios in 2007. Such enormous buying power comes dangerously close to constituting what the Justice Department calls a monopsony—control of a market by a single buyer—and it allows the giant retailer to effectively dictate the terms of trade. While Wal-Mart may not use its clout to advance any political agenda or social engineering objective, Walmart does use DVDs to lure in customers who, while they pass through the store, may buy more profitable items, such as toys, clothing, or electronics. For this task, Walmart's concern with the content of DVDs is that they not offend important customers—especially mothers—by containing material that may be inappropriate for children. Hence its "decency policy" that consigns DVDs containing sexually related nudity to "adult sections" of the store, which greatly reduces their sales. (Wal-Mart is less concerned with vulgar behavior and language.) These guidelines, in turn, put studios under tremendous pressure to sanitize their films of nudity.

Finally, movies with nudity are a problem for the studios' other main moneymaker: television. As became abundantly clear in the controversy surrounding Janet Jackson's wardrobe malfunction at Super Bowl XXXVIII, broadcast television is a government-regulated enterprise. When the government grants a free license to a station to broadcast over the public airwaves, it does so under the condition that it conform to the rules enforced by the Federal Communications Commission. Among those rules is the standard of "public decency," which among other things specifically prohibits salacious nudity, which is why CBS had to pay a fine for Ms. Jackson's brief exposure. Because the FCC regulates broadcast television (though not cable television), television stations run similar risks and embarrassments—if they show movies that include even partially nudity.

So, before a studio can license such a movie to a broadcast network, it first has to cut out all the nudity and other scenes that run afoul of the decency standard. Aside from the expense involved, it requires the hassle of obtaining the director's permission, which is contractually required by the Directors Guild of America. The same is true in studio sales to foreign television companies, which have their own government censorship.

Since graphic sex in movies is a triple liability, the studios can be expected to increasingly find that the artistic gain that comes from including it does not compensate for the financial pain and green-light fewer and fewer movies that present this problem. We may live in an anything-goes age, but if a studio wants to make money, it has to limit how much of "anything"—at least anything sexually explicit—it shows on the big screen. As one studio executive with an MBA lamented, "We may have to leave sex to the independents." In the New Hollywood, as far as studios are concerned, no nudes is good news.

THE VANISHING BOX OFFICE

The regular movie audience has been so decimated over the past six decades that the habitual weekly adult moviegoer will soon qualify, if not as an endangered species, as a niche group. In 1948, 65 percent of the population went to a movie house in an average week; in 2008, under 6 percent of the population went to see a movie in an average week.

What changed in the interval was that virtually every American family bought a TV set. In 1948, when home TV was still a rarity, theaters sold 4.6 billion tickets. By 1958, TV had penetrated most American homes, and theaters sold only 2 billion tickets. The Hollywood studios tried to counter television with technology dazzle, including wider screens (CinemaScope), noisier speakers (surround sound), and more visually exciting special effects, but technology did nothing to stem the mass defections. They also tried epic, three-hour movies, such as *Ben Hur, Lawrence of Arabia*, and *Dr. Zhivago*, that, although they succeeded individually, had little effect on the weekly movie audience. Even the much-heralded fantasy bonanzas of Spielberg and Lucas could not halt the decline. By 1988, ticket sales hovered at 1 billion.

The studios, realizing that they could no longer count on habitual moviegoers to fill theaters, devised a new strategy: creating audiences de novo for each movie via paid advertising.

Audience-creation is a very expensive enterprise—in 2007 the studios' average cost for advertising a film was $35.9 million. Studios justified this expenditure on the grounds that huge opening-weekend audiences would help turn a movie into an "event," generating word-of mouth and other free advertising that would continue to bring moviegoers into theaters, and, later, into video stores. *Titanic*, for example, took in only a modest $28 million over its opening weekend. Two weeks later, after it had become a word-of-mouth event, the movie had earned $149 million. It wound up grossing a phenomenal $600 million at American theaters. Such "event" films are what studios depend upon to pay the bills.

What terrified top studio executives in 2000 was the dearth of word-of-mouth event movies. "Word of mouth is no longer a factor," Thomas McGrath, a former Paramount vice president explained. Instead, studio marketing chiefs tried for big opening numbers by driving with a drumbeat of TV ads the one audience they can rely on: male teens. While with $36 million of ads they can still manufacture weekend teen audiences, they can no longer create the event movies that the studios need. Meanwhile, studios had to contend with thew quantum leap in quality in high-definition DVDs, television sets, and digital recorders eroding the edge multiplexes had over home entertainment in providing a movie experience. The introduction of streaming in the second decade of the 21st century was the beginning of the end of the battle to create audiences for multiplexes. It gave couch potatoes the convenience of watching movies and television anywhere and anytime by paying a monthly subscription fee. .

Studio executives slowly came to grips with the reality that they had as much chance of reversing the secular shift of audiences from the theater to streaming venues as King Canute had in commanding the tide to recede.

But what alternative do they have? The skill that movie executives have honed over the years is audience creation for multiplexes. Most of the thousands of people employed at Hollywood studios in 2009 were involved in marketing and PR departments. They justified spending $30 to 50 million per film to herd teens to the multiplexes in in hope that they could lure mass audiences out of their homes. They could see that streaming had changed the game but to abandon that hope means the end of Hollywood as they had known it.

THE REEL SILVER LINING

The public most often sees Hollywood through the lens of paparazzi cameras and the PR wires of publicists as a wildly extravagant, if not recklessly wasteful, place from which stars, accompanied by personal entourages, fly to lavish parties in private jets. But there is a less profligate side to Hollywood: the culture of the suits, in which the tight-fisted executives who run the studios pride themselves on their ability to pinch pennies out of movie budgets and wring profits out of unlikely places. Consider, for example, the profits studios found in their graveyards of dead prints. Up until the mid-1980s the initial opening of a movie required only several hundred prints—*Star Wars*, for example, opened in 1977 on only thirty-two screens. Nowadays, with simultaneous global openings, it takes 5,000 to 10,000 prints to open major movies. The 2009 sequel in Warner Bros.' Batman franchise, *The Dark Knight*, for example, which played on over 9,000 screens in the US alone, required 12,000 prints for its worldwide distribution, each costing about $1,500. Studios order the prints for these immense runs from film labs and then deduct their cost from the first revenues that flow in from the theaters. So the film production company, which is almost always set up as a separate business entity, absorbs the cost on its books. Then after a brief shelf life of a few weeks in the multiplexes, almost all the prints—except for a few hundred sent to theaters on military bases—are scrapped.

But studios found in this mounting scrap heap a literal silver lining. Each shredded print contains a small quantity of silver, which the studios can "mine" via a recovery process and sell. Silver mining, to be sure, is not a new pursuit in Hollywood. Much of the studios' pre1950s libraries, including many of the irreplaceable negatives of its classics, were destroyed to recover the silver. But with rising precious metal prices—silver exceeded $30 an ounce on the commodity market in November 2011—and hundreds of thousands of dead prints to mine, it provides a rich vein of extra income for the studios (which is not returned to the film production companies charged for the prints). Even though the proceeds studios recover from prints may amount to little more than "pocket money," as a Paramount executive described it, it fulfills a vital requisite for the suit culture: finding new sources of income.

That game ended when multiplexes converted from analog to digital projection and prints themselves are no longer necessary.

GROSS MISUNDERSTANDING

The vast preponderance of news reporting about Hollywood still concerns the weekly box-office race. It is offered free to the media every Sunday afternoon by Nielsen EDI at a low-point in its news cycle, packaged with quotes by industry sources and punning headlines by the wire services, so it can be reported as if it were a high-stakes horse race. In fact, it is, to borrow Daniel Boorstin's concept, a weekly pseudo-event whose sole purpose of the release of is to garner media attention. Once upon a time, six decades ago, such box-office numbers were critical to the fortunes of Hollywood. The major studios then owned most of the large theater chains and made virtually all their profits from ticket sales at their own theaters. But beginning in the late 1940s, the Hollywood studios were forced to divest their theaters, and they became organized in multiplex chains that the studios did not control. As television sets, DVD players, and streaming became ubiquitous in American homes, the studios were forced to radically change their business model, moving their profit centers from large to the small screen, making the box-office race even less relevant..

Even the numbers themselves are misleading The reported "grosses" are not those of the studios but the projected sales of tickets at the movie houses in the US and Canada (which is counted by Hollywood as part of the U.S.) Whatever the amount actually is, movie houses remit about 50 percent to the movie distributor, which then deducts, off the top, its out-of-pocket of costs, which includes advertising, prints, insurance, local taxes, and other logistical expenses. These off-the-top deduction for an average big studio movie now amount to about $37 million. So, just to stay in the black, a movie would need $74 million in ticket sales. Even many films that are #1 may not wind up with much from the box-office. For example, Disney, which hailed as a great success the nearly a quarter-billion-dollar "gross" of its movie Gone In 60 Seconds, wound up with only $11 million from theaters, and since it cost $103.3 million to make the movie, it was in the red. This is not uncommon. Most Hollywood movies nowadays actually lose money at the American box-office and make it from ancillary markets.

The outcome of the box-office race also has little importance to theaters these days because each of the major multiplex chains e book all the studios' wide-released movies. It does not matter to them if Movie A, B, or C win because they have them all playing on their screens. Their only concern is the total number of people who come and how much popcorn, and soda they buy. Even though every week some movie will finish first, the total audience can shrink, as it has been shrinking since 1949.

The studios, which are also the distributors, concern is the cumulative revenue their movies take in over many platforms, including both domestic and foreign movie houses, DVD stores, pay TV output deals, and TV licensing. A movie that is number one at the box office can fare very badly in its cumulative results.

Consider for example, h Paramount's *Sahara,* which I served as an expert witness in a lawsuit involving its finances. Although it was #1 at the box-office, it would up becoming one of the biggest money-losers in history. On the other hand, movies that finish at the bottom of the weekly pile, , such as Woody Allen's *Midnight In Paris,* Wes Anderson's *Moonrise Kingdom* ,and Darren Arronofsky's *Black Swan,* can ultimately take in more money than movies that finish ahead of them. It certainly helps to be first on a weekend, but not all weekends are equally valuable.   There are holiday weekends which produce ten times as much revenue as others in the slack season (when teen-agers return to school). A Fourth of July second or third place movie can take in far money than a first place finish in October, since the total pie is so much larger. And films that open in the summer, no matter where they finish, will also arm more than Fall films from Xmas DVD sales, since there is a 4-5 month embargo on the release of movies on DVD.   Nor does the box-office race necessarily affect foreign revenues, which now are more important than domestic revenue. For major movies, such as Avatar, over 70 percent of the theatrical revenue is from overseas.

Nor does the box-office race provide a fair measure of popular taste since it lumps together movies that open on thousands of screens with those that choose to open on a few dozen screens with a strategy of benefitting from reviews and word-of mouth. Consider, for example, that *Moonrise Kingdom,* which on May 25th 2012 opened on only four screens in two cities, and finished last at the race with MIB 3, which opened on 4,248 screens, and finished #1 that weekend, Is there any meaningful comparison of their appeal? MIB3 was dead after 3 weeks, while *Moonrise Kingdom* moved to 924 theaters, and is still, after 16 weeks, drawing audiences to theaters. What a box-office victory actually measures is the size of the opening and the efficacy of the studio's marketing arm in getting people to go to a movie on a Friday night largely on the basis of 30-second snippets with which they have been bombarded five to seven times the previous week. This is a job the studios do amazingly well, but it has little to say about the intrinsic appeal of the movie.

To be sure, the race produces bragging rights every week for the winning studio's marketing department, which then exploit the "Number # 1" title in newspaper ads (for which studios spend on average about $4 million per title.) As the publicity derived from this game further enhances the studios revenue, their motivation is clear in promoting the race.

But why does the media play along in the promotion. The reason is not a lack of diligence or intelligence on the part of journalists, it is the only "news" available in an entertainment news cycle, which generally requires a story about Hollywood to be linked to an interesting current event. And in light of the brief time frame surrounding the opening of movie, it is the only game available. Any real digging into the economics of a movie would take considerable time since studios tightly seal all the relevant information, such as the terms of distribution deals, financing, subsidies, and stars' compensation, through Non-Disclosure Agreements. Even extras are NDA-ed (as I found out when I was an extra in Wall Street 2). So the box-office race provides the path of least resistance for journalists

The problem here is that the media's fixation on the box office race diverts its attention from the on-going transformation of Hollywood's business. It neglects the reality that today the six major studios get less than 15 percent of the total revenue from showing their movies in American movie houses. Most of their most of their money comes from another, nearly invisible source: licensing their intellectual properties. Each studio has a vast libraries of thousands of movies, animated shorts, and TV series it licenses out. The principle licensees are worldwide cable networks, pay-tv, and broadcast television. A top executive at Time Warner recently did the math for me to demonstrate that between 85 percent and 90 percent of its entertainment earnings comes from licensing its movies and television show to television. It is more or less the same story at the four other largest studios. The reason that licensing is so immensely profitable is that, unlike movie house distribution, studios do not have to pay advertising, print, or logistic costs. Almost all the money received, except for the residuals that are paid to guild pension plans, goes toes the bottom line. The same is true with the rise of streaming in 2009. Studios initially cashed in on this new business by licensing their films in their libraries to streamers, such as Hulu, Netflix, Apple and Amazon. As they jacked up their fees, however, the streamers began producing their own content.

Hollywood's money machine depends on the retaining studios' absolute control over these intellectual properties; a requisite, which, will be critically challenged by streamers who not only produce their own content but keep all ancillary rights.

The screenwriter William Goldman famously explained the economics of Hollywood this way: nobody knows anything. The issue for journalists is why it is largely misunderstood. The box-office race that is spoon-fed to them may entertain journalists' audience every week, but by neglecting the changing economics of Hollywood, and the politics that flow from it, they also leave their audience, much like a movie audience, in the dark about what is really shaping Hollywood.

PART II
STAR CULTURE

THE CONTRACT'S THE THING— IF NOT FOR HAMLET, FOR ARNOLD SCHWARZENEGGER

The nonstop anecdotes that stars give in celebrity interviews about the stunts they supposedly performed, their favorite hobbies, and how much they enjoyed working with other stars may serve to hype their latest project—a job they are contractually required to do—but they evade a central issue: the art of the deal has come to replace the art of movies. To understand how the new Hollywood really works, one need only read stars' contracts. Consider, for example, Governor Arnold Schwarzenegger's agreement for *Terminator 3: The Rise of the Machines*. It's a state-of-the-art exercise in deal-making.

The contract was brilliantly put together by the Hollywood super-lawyer Jacob Bloom between June 2000 and December 2001, requiring no fewer than twenty-one drafts, and runs thirty-three pages including appendices. For starters, Schwarzenegger got a $29.25 million "pay or play" fee, meaning he would be paid whether or not the movie was made. (At the time, that figure was a record for

guaranteed compensation.) The first $3 million would be delivered on signing and the balance during the course of nineteen weeks of "principal photography," which is the part of a production during which the actors are in front of the camera. For every week the shooting ran over its nineteen-week schedule, Schwarzenegger would receive an additional $1.6 million in "overage." Then there was the "perk package"—a lump sum of $1.5 million for private jets, a fully equipped gym trailer, three-bedroom deluxe suites on locations, round-the-clock limousines, and personal bodyguards. The producers Mario Kassar and Andrew Vajna did not agree to pay Schwarzenegger this record sum because he possessed unique acting skills—after all, the part he was to play (along with a digital double and many stuntmen) was that of a slow-speaking robot. They also did not pay Schwarzenegger on the basis of his box office track record. Indeed, his previous two films, *End of Days* (1999) and *The Sixth Day* (2000), had failed both at the world-wide box office and at video rental stores. Nevertheless, in the ten years that had elapsed since *Terminator 2: Judgment Day*, Schwarzenegger's image had become so inexorably linked in video games and TV reruns to the deadly robot that he had become the crucial element of the deal and Kassar and Vajna needed him to raise money.

To make this deal Kassar and Vajna first needed to get the rights to the moribund franchise. So, backed by the German-owned movie financier

Intermedia Films, they bought the sequel rights to the *Terminator* franchise for $14.5 million from the bankrupt Carolco Pictures and the initial producer, Gale Anne Hurd. Next, they spent another $5.2 million developing a script. That was the easy part. Now they needed $160 million in financing, which was more than any other movie had cost in those days. They had lined up three distributors: Warner Bros. would pay $51.6 million for North American rights, the Tokyo distributor Toho-Towa would pay $20 million for Japanese rights, and Sony Pictures Entertainment would pay $77.4 million for the rest of the world. (The balance would come mainly from tax shelter deals in Germany.) But all three distributors—Warner Bros., Sony, and Toho-Towa—made their financing conditional on Schwarzenegger signing on to play the robot. So: No Schwarzenegger, no money.

Kassar and Vajna had no real choice but to accept Schwarzenegger's terms if they wanted to make the movie (and, aside from reviving the franchise, they themselves would earn $10 million in producer fees if the deal went through). Schwarzenegger's demands, however, did not stop with the guarantee of $29.25 million. He also insisted on and got 20 percent of the gross receipts made by the venture from every market in the world—including movie theaters, videos, DVDs, television licensing, in-flight entertainment, game licensing, and so forth— once the movie had reached its cash breakeven point. Such "contingent compensation" is not unusual in movie contracts, but, in some cases, Hollywood accounting famously uses smoke and mirrors to make sure to define "breakeven" in such a way that a movie never reaches it. Schwarzenegger's contract, thanks to the ingenious lawyering of Jake Bloom, allowed for no such evasion.

Schwarzenegger also could decide who worked with him. The contract "pre-approval" clause gave him choice of not only the director (Jonathan Mostow) and the principal cast, but also his hairdresser (Peter Toothbal), his makeup man (Jeff Dawn), his driver (Howard Valesco), his stand-in (Dieter Rauter), his stunt double (Billy Lucas), the unit publicist (Sheryl Merin), his personal physician (Dr. Graham Waring), and his cook (Steve Hunter). Finally, Schwarzenegger had the contract structured to give him every possible tax advantage.

All the money was to be paid not to Schwarzenegger but to Oak Productions Inc., a corporate front he controlled. Oak Productions, in return, "lends" Schwarzenegger's services to the production. Since Schwarzenegger didn't get any money personally from the movie itself, he had more flexibility managing his exposure to taxes. For example, Oak Productions entered into a complex tax-reimbursement scheme with the production to help avoid additional tax liabilities that might occur abroad. In return, Schwarzenegger agreed to make himself available for eighteen weeks of principal photography, one week (on a nonexclusive basis) for rehearsals—if any were required—and five days for re-shooting. In addition, he had to make himself available for at least ten days, seven of them abroad, for promotional activities in connection with the initial theatrical release of the movie. This media work included everything from television and radio appearances to appearances at premieres and Internet chat rooms. The negotiation of this contract did not come cheaply—the legal and accounting budget for the movie was $2 million—and, by the time all of Schwarzenegger's demands were met, the budget of the film had risen to $187.3 million, making it then the most expensive independently produced movie in history. Another $90 million was spent advertising and marketing it.

Terminator 3 had a world box office gross of $433 million which, together with DVD, TV, and other rights, allowed the distributors to eke out a small profit, but Arnold Schwarzenegger, who had created his own "cash breakeven," was the big winner. In the bygone days of the studio system, the studios had exclusive contracts with their stars that allowed them to reap the profits from the images their PR machines had created. In the new Hollywood, the stars themselves reap the profit their brand names bring to a film. So it is not surprising that even after Schwarzenegger became the governor of California in 2004, his holding company protected his image rights by suing a small toy maker selling a Schwarzenegger-like bobble-head doll on the grounds that "Schwarzenegger is an instantly recognizable global celebrity whose name and likeness are worth millions of dollars and are solely his property."

Ironically, whereas Schwarzenegger was crucial to making the deal, once the *Terminator* franchise had been successfully resurrected, his acting services were no longer necessary for future sequels. In 2007, Kassar and Vajna sold the rights to the franchise to the game company Halcyon for $25 million, which produced *Terminator Salvation* in 2009, the first of three planned sequels. Even without Schwarzenegger, who was by now fighting his own budget battles as governor of California, it did almost as well as *Terminator 3* at the domestic box office, though not as well in the Asian markets.

MOVIE STARS COME IN TWO FLAVORS: $20 MILLION AND FREE

The difference between studio-made movies and independent-made movies is the former have an American distributor before they are filmed, or even green-lit, and therefore investors in them are assured that they will be shown in theaters, while the latter don't. And since it may take years of screenings, and endless trips to film festivals, before an indie film has a chance of finding an American distributor and many never do, raising money for them is a daunting challenge.

One ingenious device through which indie film producers overcome this problem is to recruit Hollywood stars who will work for them on the cheap and use their names to pre-sell the movie abroad. The same actors and actresses who quote Hollywood studios $20 million per movie will work on indie films for a small fraction of that fee. Often they accept "scale," as the Screen Actors Guild's minimum wage of $788 a day is called, or "near scale" of about $10,000 a week plus overtime. Instead of requiring private jets, luxury suites, and multimillion dollar perk packages as they do in studio films, the stars will fly on commercial flights, stay in inexpensive condos, and get the same per diem as the rest of the cast. Instead of receiving a sizable chunk of the gross receipts as they are accustomed to on studio films, for indie films stars will accept "net points" (even though they—or their agents—are no doubt familiar with David Mamet's famous observation that in Hollywood, "There is no Net"). "The total cost of a star can be less than that of running the office Xerox," explained one knowledgeable producer. The willingness of top stars—including Keanu Reeves, Mel Gibson, Jim Carrey, Will Ferrell, Drew Barrymore, Al Pacino, Angelina Jolie, Pierce Brosnan, Leonardo DiCaprio, Charlize Theron, Tobey Maguire, Demi Moore, Sean Penn, and Julia Roberts—to work for near scale in the parallel universe of indie films allows indie producers to take advantage of a star's cachet to finance the movies.

Ironically, in the era of the moguls, the Hollywood studios gained a similar advantage over stars by locking all their actors and actresses into long-term contracts in which they were paid a specified weekly salary regardless of the success of their movies. After the studio system collapsed in the late 1940s, the stars, represented by powerful talent agencies, quickly turned the tables on the studios. Now, no longer under studio contract, the stars auctioned off their services to the highest bidder from film to film.

The studios still paid for their films' publicity, but the stars now reaped the benefits of their cachet via product endorsement, licensing their images for games and toys, and a raft of other celebritized enterprises.

Despite the lure of enormous compensation from studios, which now include perk packages and cuts of the gross receipts that can easily exceed $30 million a film, stars find occasional satisfaction in working for coolie wages in indie productions, making a distinction between, as one top Creative Artists Agency (CAA) agent put it, "commerce and art." Some stars may find that roles in studio comic-book movies (that they share with live stuntmen and digital doubles) do not provide the acting opportunities, award possibilities, prestige, camaraderie, or even aura of coolness of indie productions. Others may want to work with a particular director, such as Woody Allen, Spike Jonze, or David Mamet, or burnish their fading image as an actor. They might also need to fill a hole in their schedule since, PR hype aside, there is not an endless cornucopia of $20 million parts in Hollywood. Also, when stars do "artistic" films practically pro bono they do not officially lower their $20 million quote.

Whatever the star's motives, the indie producers get, if not a free ride, a means of financing their movies through a three-step process called pre-sales. Here is how it works:

Step One. The indie producer makes a pre-sale contract with a distributor overseas. In such an arrangement, the producer usually turns over all rights to exhibit the movie—including selling DVDs and TV licenses—in a particular country in return for a minimum guarantee of money once the film is completed and delivered. The catch-22 here is that a foreign distributor often will not commit to a pre-sale contract if there is no American distributor or unless the film has a recognizable star (with a star the distributor has at least a chance of selling the DVD and TV rights). So indie producers must persuade or seduce a star into joining the movie—and here is where the genius comes in—for practically no money. With a star in tow, a producer can often make enough pre-sales to cover most, if not all, of the budget.

Step Two. Since pre-sales are no more than promissory notes, the indie producer must borrow against them from banks to pay for the movie. Before he can do that, he needs to guarantee the banks that the movie, once begun, will get finished and delivered to foreign distributors. What's needed is a completion bond, which guarantees the banks that it will pay all cost overruns necessary to finish the movie and if the production is abandoned, it will pay all the money lost on the venture, which means that one way or another the bank will get back its money. Two companies, Film Finance, Inc. and International Film Guarantors, provide almost all the completion bonds for independent productions. (Studios that internally finance their own movies do not need completion bonds.) Before either company will sell a producer a completion bond, the producer has to meet its requisites, which include buying full insurance for the star (so if he or she is injured or quits the completion bond coverer gets all the money back from the insurer) and turning over to the completion bond company the ultimate control of the budget (including the right, if anything goes wrong, to take over the production and bring in its own director to complete it). The indie producer also has to pay the company about 2 percent of the budget.

Step Three. With the completion bond in hand, and the pre-sales contracts as collateral, the producer then borrows the money from a bank or other financier. Since the completion bond companies are themselves backed by giant insurers, such as Lloyds of London and Fireman's Fund, the banks take only a very limited risk in making such loans. John W. Miller, who recently retired as head of JP Morgan Chase's movie financing unit, told me that in issuing billions of dollars in loans he did not read the scripts of the indie films he finances. "My bet is on the solvency of the distributors." When these pre-sales contracts are with established international distributors, such as Sony Pictures, Canal Plus, Toho Films, or Buena Vista International, that risk is, he said, "negligible."

Even after scaling all these hurdles, securing the money, and making the movie, the indie producer faces one further challenge: getting the movie into American multiplexes. Even with a completed movie and star, finding a distributor requires going from film festival to film festival, an odyssey that often proves unfruitful. (More than 2,000 indie films were submitted to the Sundance Film Festival in 2009, for example, of which about one percent were accepted.) However, the presence of a star greatly improve its chances, especially in those festivals, such as Cannes, Berlin, Venice, and Toronto, that depend on stars for publicity and photo-ops. As one highly successful indie producer explains, it gives the acquisition executives there more of an incentive to give the film a chance with distribution, because they figure that, even if the film is a hard sell, they can always promote the star. Selling the film ultimately is what it's all about. So the Hollywood star as *homo ludens*, or at least seeking some kind of non-monetary gratification, winds up as the crucial element in a business model that has sustained a large part of independent films—and, for that, we can all be grateful.

THE ANGST QUESTION IN HOLLYWOOD: WHAT IS YOUR CASH BREAKEVEN?

In the arcane universe of Hollywood contracts, there are two kinds of money paid to stars, directors, actors, and other participants in movies. The first kind is called "fixed compensation" and is paid out, like any other wage, when the participant does his job. The second kind is called "contingent compensation," which depends on how well the film does, is typically not paid until the revenues reach an arbitrary point artfully called "cash breakeven." Whatever percentage a participant is supposed to get, whether it is based on gross or net points, it is triggered by this contractual definition. In some contracts in lieu of the star receiving any sizable fixed compensation, the cash breakeven is set at dollar one, which means his pay kicks in immediately after the print and advertising costs are reimbursed, but usually it is set high enough to allow a studio to recover most of its production costs. Not only may the definition vary from film to film, but it is not unusual for many participants in the same film to have different cash break-evens. For each participant it is defined not by any set accounting rules but by Hollywood's prevailing Golden rule: Who has the gold makes the rules. The contentious negotiations, which center around self-serving claims about how much gold any participant might add to the venture, almost irresistibly lead to the most powerful player getting the lowest cash breakeven, which means he or she will be the first to get paid. The problem here is that the money paid first to the more powerful players is added to the cost side of the equation for everyone else, which pushes them further away from reaching their higher cash breakeven. As a result, the less powerful, which includes writers, may never qualify for their contingency payments. Woody Allen jokes in his movie *Hollywood Ending* about a director being so lowly regarded that he received "quadruple cash breakeven," and therefore the movie had to gross four times his breakeven point before he received a penny of his contingency pay. On the other hand, the handful of stars and directors who are indispensable to a movie getting green-lighted can dictate their own golden cash breakeven. And, to protect the egos of less privileged participants in the Hollywood Community, these golden cash break-evens are usually kept a closely guarded secret. But consider the golden terms Arnold Schwarzenegger got for *Terminator 3*. Brilliantly drafted by his lawyer, his cash breakeven clause specifies:

> Cash Breakeven shall be defined as the point at which there shall have been recouped from Adjusted Gross Receipts an amount equaling all actual distribution expenses attributable to the Picture (provided there shall be no double deductions for any item, including without limitation residuals), all costs of production

of the Picture (including without limitation any pre-break participations, mutually-approved deferments and completion bond fee), actual interest and actual financing costs related to the Picture, a producer fee in the aggregate amount of $5,000,000 for Andy Vajna and Mario Kassar and an overhead charge to Intermedia Film Equities Limited equal to ten percent (10 percent) of the bonded budget (with no interest on overhead or overhead on interest). For purposes of calculating Cash Breakeven only, Adjusted Gross Receipts shall include a 100 percent home video royalty (i.e. home video revenues less costs, provided no such costs shall be deducted if such costs were previously deducted hereunder) to the extent that Producer is accounted by distributors at a 100 percent home video royalty or if Producer is not accounted for at a 100 percent home video royalty, with respect to any Adjusted Gross Receipts, such Adjusted Gross Receipts shall include and be calculated with a home video royalty equal to the home video royalty Producer receives with respect to such Adjusted Gross Receipts, but in no event less than a 35 percent home video royalty. For all other purposes (other than calculating Cash Breakeven), including the calculation of [Schwarzenegger] Participation and the Deferred Participation, Adjusted Gross Receipts shall include a 35 percent home video royalty, or if the agreement for the services of the director of the Picture so provides, then such greater home video royalty shall be included in the Adjusted Gross Receipts of the Picture for purposes of calculating [Schwarzenegger] Participation and the Deferred Participation.

Take video and DVD sales, for example. Under the standard Hollywood contract, studios credit the film with a video "royalty" equal only to 20 percent of the sales. That means that if sales of a DVD total $20 million, only $4 million of that is counted toward reaching the breakeven point. In the case of DVD and video royalties, the contract specifies: "For purposes of calculating Cash Breakeven only, Adjusted Gross Receipts shall include a 100

Budget Based on Script Dated November 9th,2001

100 Days MAIN UNIT PHOTOGRAPHY
63 Loc LA/37 LA Stage/

RECEIVED

60 DAYS SECOND UNIT
45 Days Full
15 Reduced

File: T3 Master Budget Friday,

7 DAYS AERIAL UNIT
Prepared: Feb 12, 2002

Commence Pre-Production: Nov 12th
Commence Photography: April 15
Answer Print: April 15t, 2003 S

Post Production: 27 Weeks

DRAFT - CONFIDENTIAL

CRITICAL ASSUMPTION- LAST
OF SHOOTING ARE ON STAGES

Acct#	Category Title	Page	Total
1100	STORY & RIGHTS	1	$19,569,305
1200	PRODUCER & STAFF	1	$10,033,210
1300	DIRECTOR & STAFF	4	$5,006,254
1400	TALENT	5	$34,565,248
1500	ATL TRAVEL & LIVING	19	$0
1900	TOTAL ATL FRINGES		$1,312,848
	Total Above-The-Line		**$70,475,801**
2000	PRODUCTION STAFF	19	$1,954,390
2150	EXTRA TALENT	26	$395,603
2200	ART DEPARTMENT	29	$1,613,334
2300	SET CONSTRUCTION	37	$6,654,815
2500	SET OPERATIONS	45	$2,820,576
2600	SPECIAL EFFECTS	53	$4,494,422
2700	SET DRESSING	57	$2,422,254
2800	ACTION PROPS	62	$776,518
3000	WARDROBE	64	$1,638,375
3000	PICT. VEH. & ANIMALS	68	$1,479,725
3100	MAKEUP & HAIR	72	$555,812
3200	ELECTRICAL	74	$3,579,571
3300	CAMERA	77	$2,419,864
3400	SOUND	82	$358,885
3500	TRANSPORTATION	84	$3,953,281
3600	LOCATION	100	$4,361,743
3700	FILM & LAB	111	$1,030,505
3800	VIDEO TAPE	112	$184,498
3900	CREATURE EFFECTS	113	$3,196,000
4000	FACILITY EXPENSES	114	$1,977,450
4100	TESTS	114	$60,000
4200	SECOND UNIT	115	$5,148,117
4300	AERIAL UNIT	136	$256,731
4400	SPECIAL PHOTOGRAPHY	139	$319,091
4500	COMPUTER GRAPHICS	139	$200,793
4900	TOTAL BTL FRINGES		$6,609,473
	Total Production		**$57,446,342**
5000	EDITING & PROJECTION	141	$2,312,563
5100	VIDEO TAPE POST	148	$288,552
5200	MUSIC	149	$1,836,164
5300	SOUND (POST PRODUCTION)	150	$691,493
5400	VISUAL EFFECTS	152	$19,885,650
5600	FILM, TAPE, & LIBRARY	154	$301,683
5700	TITLES & OPTICALS	155	$142,500
5900	TOTAL POST FRINGES		$584,482
	Total Post Production		**$26,047,087**
6500	PUBLICITY	155	$141,500
6700	INSURANCE	156	$2,000,000
6900	GENERAL EXPENSES	156	$1,796,151
6900	COMPLETION BOND FEE		$2,382,565
7000	CONTINGENCY		$7,000,000
7200	TOTAL OTHER FRINGES		$30,668
	Total Other		**$13,360,904**
	TOTAL ABOVE-THE-LINE		**$70,475,801**
	TOTAL BELOW-THE-LINE		**$96,844,333**
	TOTAL ABOVE & BELOW-THE-LINE		**$167,320,333**
	GRAND TOTAL		**$167,320,333**

Where does Hollywood's money go? See the budget for *Terminator 3* above. The internal breakdown of this budget is over 100 pages. percent home video royalty (i.e. home video revenues less costs)." So unlike weaker players, Schwarzenegger could count all the money taken in from DVDs and video, $20 million, less their actual cost, toward reaching the threshold where he gets his cut. Of course these payments to Schwarzenegger effectively came at the expense of less powerful talent (like writers) with higher breakeven points. But that is part of the contract game. But alas the studios' cash break even game has no future if the streamers take over Hollywood production. With them, there are no DVDs, no TV syndication, no separate foreign markets. Since they buy all the rights, there is no back end.

THE SAD LESSON OF NICOLE KIDMAN'S KNEE—OR WHAT A STAR NEEDS TO GET A PART

A star must be insurable. Cast insurance is the sine qua non for a movie to be financed. A production company cannot get a completion bond, which financing institutions insist on, unless it has insurance coverage for the star, especially if the star is deemed an "essential element" of the film. With it, if the star dies, becomes disabled or ill, refuses to perform, or abandons the film, the insurer agrees to cover the resulting loss—which may be the entire investment in the project. For example, if anything had happened to Arnold Schwarzenegger in *Terminator 3*, the insurers would have had to pay in excess of $150 million. (The insurance for *Terminator 3* was $2 million.)

For their part, insurers attempt to reduce their exposure to disaster by deciding whom not to insure. They not only evaluate the past history and claim pattern of stars, but they require many levels of medical examination and drug sampling before and during shooting. They may also place restrictions on activities—such as stunts—and assign "watchers" on the set to make sure that stars honor those restrictions. If stars present too great a risk, insurers can elect either to make the premiums prohibitively high or to refuse to insure them altogether.

Nicole Kidman is a case in point. Kidman injured her knee during the filming of *Moulin Rouge* in Australia in 2000, resulting in a $3-million insurance loss, and then quit *Panic Room* in 2001, leading to the insurer having to pay some $7 million for the replacement actress (Jodie Foster). As a result, her public and critical acclaim notwithstanding, Miramax was initially unable to get insurance on her for its film *Cold Mountain*, which had a budget approaching $100 million. From the perspective of the insurer, Fireman's Fund, she was a definite risk. As an insurance executive noted in an email, "While the doctors who did her surgery and her current knee doctor can say she is fully recovered, the fact remains that the doctor we sent her to for her examination noted swelling in the knee." The executive goes on: "The other major fact that can't be changed is our paying three claims for this actress's knees over the years."

To get the necessary policy from Fireman's Fund, Kidman agreed to put $1 million of her own salary in an escrow account that would be forfeited if she failed to maintain the production schedule, and she agreed to use a stunt double for all scenes that the insurer considered potentially threatening to her knee. In addition, the co-producer, Lakeshore Entertainment, added another $500,000 to the escrow account. Only after the completion-bond company, International Film Guarantors, certified that "Kidman is fully aware that she must get through this picture without a problem," adding, "She fully understands this and will not allow anything to get in the way of her finishing this picture"—did she get her insurance—and her role in *Cold Mountain*. Having made the all-important move from borderline uninsurable to borderline insurable, she could make movies again. No matter how great their acting skills and box office drawing power, stars cannot get lead roles if they are uninsurable. Great acting skills and box office drawing power may make the star, but insurance is what it takes to make the movie.

THE STARLET'S DILEMMA

"Everything's geared to fifteen-year-olds . . . I have girlfriends who are twenty-five in L.A. who are lying about their age because people tell them they're too old. That's how pathetic it is."
　　—Morgan Fairchild

In Hollywood, where the radioactive half-life of a starlet's fame may be briefer than her high school education, the effective career of an actress can be nasty, brutish, and short, or, in the lingo, "way harsh." The opportunities for a pretty starlet in the romantic comedies, horror films, and the amusement-park films that are made for the Clearasil crowd tend to dry up when they hit thirty, one of Hollywood's most insightful producers told me. They have to start acting "as opposed to simply gracing the screen with their gorgeous presence and many of those starlets are just not equipped for this second step." Anti-aging camouflage, such as plastic surgery, Botox, collagen injections, and other elixirs may provide a brief respite but eventually every actress comes up against the age stereotyping in Hollywood famously described by

Goldie Hawn: There are only three ages for women: Babe, District Attorney, and *Driving Miss Daisy*. Some actresses succeed in breaking through this age barrier but even they find it a daunting challenge to escape Hollywood's requisite and satisfy the youth culture, as Rosanna Arquette demonstrates in her interviews with Meg Ryan, Holly Hunter, Charlotte Rampling, Sharon Stone, Whoopi Goldberg, Martha Plimpton, and a score of other actresses in her 2002 documentary *Searching For Debra Winger*. Equally illuminating are Nancy Ellison's photographs in *Starlets: Before They Were Famous* of gorgeously posed actresses who, having failed to make it through the Babe portal, vanished from Hollywood. As Martha Plimpton explains about casting, "It's either, she's a starlet or she's an old hag." Such ageism proceeds not from malice, ignorance, or disdain for the performers on the part of studio executives, but from their business model.

When studios found that they could no longer count on habitual moviegoers to fill theaters, they went into the very risky business of creating tailor-made audiences for each and every movie they released. Like in an election campaign, the studios had to get people to turn out at the multiplexes on a specific date—the opening weekend. The principal means of generating this audience is to buy ads on national television. For this strategy to work efficiently, the studios find a target audience that predictably clusters around programs on which they can afford to buy time. They then bombard this audience—usually seven times in the preceding week to an opening—with thirty-second eye-catching ads.

The studios zero in on teens not because they necessarily like them, or even because the teens buy buckets of popcorn, but because they are the only demographic group that can be easily motivated to leave their home. Even though lassoing this teen herd is enormously expensive—over $30 million a film—the studios profit from the fact that this young audience is also the coin of the realm for merchandisers such as McDonald's, Domino's, and Pepsi. The studios depend upon these companies for tie-deals that can add a hundred million dollars or more in advertising to a single film and can expand the primary audience for DVDs, video games, and other licensable properties on which the studios now bank on for their economic survival. Studios therefore place the lion's share of their TV advertising—over 80 percent in 2005—on the cable and network programs that are watched primarily by people under twenty-five. The studios also incorporate music in their sound tracks that teenagers listen to and try to cast the sort of babe-actresses that their crucial audience can relate to, if not fantasize about. Adrienne Shelley, the star of *The Unbelievable Truth*, for example, described her casting experience this way: "I get a call in my car on the way to an audition from the agent. He said, 'What is really important is that they think you are fuckable.'"

Of course, for the ex-babe actress who is no longer able or willing to play this Hollywood game, there is always the possibility of starring in foreign and independent movies, especially if her name helps raise money abroad. But while roles in these more adult-oriented movies may be more artistically rewarding than roles as fantasy-bait in teen movies, they are rarely, if ever, as high-paying.

THERE IS NO NET

Unlike the dozen or so powerful star actors, directors and producers, such as Tom Cruise, Steven Spielberg, and Jerry Bruckheimer, who get a cut of the gross revenue of a movie, regardless of whether the movie is in the red or black, most creative people who produce, write, direct, or act in movies get, in addition to their upfront fees, a percentage of the net profits, called "net points." No matter how much the movie seems to take in at the box office, these so-called "net players" rarely ever see a penny from their net points. The frustration that runs rife in Hollywood social circles is summed up in David Mamet's *Speed-the-Plow* when the lead character says that what he has learned about the movie business is "There is no net!"

The reason net players realize little more than psychic income from their "points" is that studios set up each movie as a separate off-the-books corporation designed to produce revenue for the gross players, which include the studio itself since it takes a dollar-one distribution fee of up to 30 percent of the gross and an overhead fee of fifteen percent gross; equity partners who often are given direct cuts, called "corridors," into discreet portions of the gross, and offset their financial risks; and any stars who are gross players. After these cuts, and the costs and interest (10 percent per annum) are deducted, there rarely is anything in the net pie.

Consider, for example, what happened with the revenue from Disney's 2000 *Gone in 60 Seconds*, which was cited in Disney's annual report as a smash hit. Produced by Jerry Bruckheimer, one of the top producers in Hollywood, and starring Nicholas Cage and Angelina Jolie, the teen car-crash movie cost $103.3 million to make and took in $242 million at the box office. While someone unfamiliar with Mamet's dictum might assume that those holding net points—including the director Dominic Sena, the screenplay writer Scott Rosenberg, and Angelina Jolie—might get a pay-off, here is what happened to the nearly half-billion in revenues it generated at the box office.

Of that $242 million in ticket sales, the theaters kept $139.8 million or nearly 60 percent. So even though Disney's distribution arm, Buena Vista International, is probably Hollywood's most powerful distributor, it got only $102.2 million or about 40 percent of the world box office. From that sum, it deducted $90.6 million for out-of-pocket distribution expenses, which included $67.4 million for buying the ads necessary to reach a global teenage audience, $13 million for prints, and $10.2 million for insurance, shipping, custom fees, check collection, and local taxes, and this left an adjusted gross of just $11.6 million. And from this, the gross players, including Buena Vista (which had a 30 percent distribution fee), Cage, and Bruckheimer, got another $3.4 million. At this point, after the theatrical release, the $103.4 million movie was about $95 million in the red.

In the age of streaming not only is there no net but there is no reporting on the financial performance of a movie. Since streamers charge monthly subscription fees to viewers no matter how few or how many films or TV episodes they watch, the do not have to report on the numbers individual films or TV programs generate. And as they don't give directors, producers, actors, writers or any other participant the right to share in the revenue they produce, they don't share the data with them.

THE END OF THE VIDEO WINDFALL

Six months after the theatrical release, *Gone in 60 Seconds* was released in video stores, and garnered about $198 million in sales. But only a small fraction of this sum, $39.6 million, was credited to the movie because, according to the standard industry contract, it was entitled to only a 20 percent royalty of Buena Vista Home Entertainment's total video and DVD revenues. The $158.4 million balance went to Disney's home entertainment division. From the movie's share of $39.6 million, the distributor deducted

THE RISE OF DVDS

MPA Studio Revenues from DVD vs. VHS
Studio receipts
(Billions of dollars)

Year	DVD	VHS	Total
1993	0	5.9	5.9
1997	0	9.8	9.8
2002	10.39	5.929	16.3
2003	14.9	3.9906	18.9
2004	18.8	2.1	20.9

2005	20.8	.6	21.4
2006	19.1	.2	19.3
2007*	17.8	.1	17.9

* The studios stopped furnishing these revenue numbers to the MPA in 2008.

$19.7 million for its expenses and fee. The star Nicholas Cage, who had 5 percent of the gross, then got $3.9 million, leaving the movie with only $16 million from the video stores. So even with the video windfall, the movie was still nearly $80 million in the hole.

The net revenue flow came one year later from the pay-tv channels, which paid $18.2 million, which was top dollar because of its box office success. From that Disney deducted $2.7 million to pay the residuals to actors and unions, and $149,000 for insurance and other expenses. So another $15.4 million was credited to the movie, which would have reduced the movie's deficit to about $63 million, if it were not for the gross players cuts that were added to the deficit and the 10 percent per year interest. As a result of these charges, even with further TV licensing money trickling in, by 2008, *Gone in 60 Seconds* was $155 million in the red. And even with a half-billion gross, the net players would not see a penny.

Disney, which raked in a large percent of the nearly half-billion gross through its ownership of Buena Vista International and Buena Vista Home Entertainment, of course made money, despite the paper losses in its off the-books entity for *Gone in 60 Seconds*. The net players of course all got paid their fixed compensation. They had willingly agreed to the terms in their contract, which defined their net, and their contracts were almost certainly vetted by their talent agents, business managers, and lawyers, who deal day in and day out with similar contracts. So if the net players are deceived by the contractual definition of net profits, it is, like so many other aspects of Hollywood relationships, a self-deception. They want to believe, no matter what their lawyers, agents, and business managers tell them, that they will participate in the profits of their product.

Such video windfalls will not continue in the age of streaming. Netflix, Disney Plus, HBO Max and other streaming services eliminate the need to buy and store videos, DVDs and Blu-rays. And as Hollywood studios shift from theatrical distribution to streaming, as Disney is doing, fewer movies will even be available on these stored media.

NOBODY GETS GROSS

Hollywood studios never give participants—not even ones as powerful as Arnold Schwarzenegger, Tom Cruise, Tom Hanks, Jerry Bruckenheimer, Steven Spielberg, or even Pixar Animation Studios—an unadulterated percentage of the box office gross, or the video store gross, or any other retail gross. As one top Viacom executive explained, "The first truism of Hollywood is: Nobody gets gross—not even a top first dollar gross player."

What the top gross players do get are two kinds of compensation: fixed and contingent. The fixed part is the up-front money that gross players are paid whatever happens to the movie. The contingent part is the percentage of a pool—called the "distributor's adjusted gross" in Hollywood lawyer lingo—that the players get after certain conditions are met, such as the movie earning back the amount of fixed compensation or reaching a contractually-defined cash breakeven point. The pool is "filled" with the money that the distribution arm collects or, in the case of DVDs, gets credited with. With movies, the pool (eventually) gets the remittance from theaters left over after the theater owners deduct their share of ticket sales and house allowance and after the distributor deducts off the top expenses, such as check collection, currency transfers, stamp taxes, duties, and trade association fees.

To see how these gross participations work in practice, look again at Arnold Schwarzenegger's thirty-three page contract for *Terminator 3*, which is still considered the gold standard for the super-gross players. For his fixed compensation, Schwarzenegger received $29.25 million—then a record sum. He got the first $3 million on signing and the balance during the course of principal photography. His contingent compensation was 20 percent of the adjusted gross receipts of the distributors (Warner Bros. in the US, Sony Pictures and Intermedia abroad). The adjusted part of the equation allowed the studio to deduct the items specified on page three of the contract: All industry-standard and customary off-the top exclusions and deductions, i.e. checking, collection conversion costs, quota costs, trade association fees, residuals, and taxes. Schwarzenegger's lawyer Jacob Bloom is without peer in the entertainment business, but the best he could do here was to cap some of the collection charges at $250,000; he could not touch the residuals or tax deduction. Bloom did manage to get the all-important DVD royalty contribution to the pool raised to 35 percent (although only for Schwarzenegger). As good as this was, it meant that Schwarzenegger was entitled to only 7 percent of what the studios took in from their DVD sales.

Schwarzenegger's contingent compensation would not kick in until the film met the breakeven point defined in the contract. Although the film achieved a $428 million world box office gross, it just barely reached its cash breakeven point, so, alas, Governor Schwarzenegger has earned only a pittance so far from his gross participation beyond his $29.25 million payday. Tom Cruise got a more immediate slice of the action for *Mission Impossible 2*. In return for his producing, acting, guaranteeing against cost overruns, and paying other gross players their share—including Director John Woo's 7.5 percent—Cruise's production company got 30 percent of Paramount's adjusted gross receipts.

In this light, Peter Jackson's compensation for *King Kong* was a relative bargain. Universal paid $20 million in fixed compensation to Jackson's production company not only for his directing services, but also for the script writing and producing services of his collaborators Fran Walsh and Philippa Boyens. And, making a sweet deal even sweeter, the New Zealand citizenship of Jackson and his team qualified Universal for a cash subsidy from the New Zealand government that could be as high as $20 million (and, by itself, that subsidy could pay Jackson's entire fixed compensation). In addition, once the fixed compensation is earned back, Jackson's company also got 20 percent of Universal's adjusted gross receipts, which means it got at least an additional $20 million from movie rentals (which now have passed $200 million worldwide) as well as a huge payoff from future DVDs and television rights.

Such deals are costly, but not crazy. The studios' business nowadays is entirely driven by huge franchises that serve as worldwide licensing platforms. And the most predictable rainmakers for these windfalls, such as Steven Spielberg, George Lucas, Tom Cruise, Jerry Bruckenheimer, and Peter Jackson, are all gross players represented by savvy lawyers and agents who know all the ropes of the movie business. To be sure, not all of their projects turn out to be billion-dollar franchises, but they have little downside. Look at *King Kong*: The upside for Universal was a licensing franchise that would enrich the studio with billions in revenues for years to come. But even if that gamble fails and there are no ape sequels, the studio lost little, if any money, on the movie itself. In this topsy-turvy world, it makes perfect sense for the studios to recruit the best gross players, as long as the gross they give away is not really the gross.

The age of streaming drastically changes this equation. Streamers do not need these huge sums to star directors because, unlike the Hollywood rights model, they are not looking to create licensing franchises. Instead, they need show runners to create multiple season series, such as Breaking Bad or The Crown, which will keeps subscribers.

"I DO MY OWN STUNTS"

Nowhere does Hollywood's culture of deception more clearly manifest itself than on those television talk shows in which stars talk about their movies. The point of this media exercise, at least for the studios releasing the movies, is to fuse the celebrity stars with their fictive movie characters (otherwise the stars might focus interest on themselves instead of the movies being opened). So carefully-designed PR scripts require that the stars "stay in character," as Hollywood calls real life play-acting. When it comes to action movies, the scenario typically calls for stars to tell making-of-movie anecdotes that suggest that they, like the heroes they play on screen, perform death-defying feats. Even if the putative perils are an obvious stretch, they can almost invariably count on a suspension of disbelief on the part of their host-interrogator. Consider, for example, the heroics related on MTV by the three lovely stars of *Charlie's Angels: Full Throttle*, Lucy Liu, Drew Barrymore, and Cameron Diaz. The MTV interviewer, JC Chasez began by asking, "Did you guys do any of your own stunts?"

"We did," Lucy Liu ("Alex") jumps in.

"We get to do all these amazing things," Cameron Diaz ("Natalie") adds, describing by way of example how Drew Barrymore ("Dylan") clung to a speeding car going about "35 miles an hour" while "hitting on the hood of the car"—even after her safety cord came undone. "She's literally hanging on to the car," Liu explains.

At this point in the story, with Barrymore precariously holding onto the hood with one hand and banging on it with the other, the interviewer asks her excitedly why she didn't yell, "Cut"?

Barrymore ("Dylan") explains despite the danger to herself, she persevered with the shot because "you get so into the adrenaline and you want to be tough. . . . my character, Dylan, was trying to stop the bad guy." In other words, she had morphed into Dylan—at least in the PR script.

Now back to reality. Stars may have license on talk shows to fantasize about performing perilous stunts such as hanging off the hood of a speeding car, but on a movie set, no matter how willing they may be to risk their lives and limbs, studios will not permit them to take such risks for two reasons.

First, stars often do not have an opportunity to perform stunts because action movies are not shot linearly. The filming is divided between a first unit, "principal photography," that shoots the stars and other actors, and the "second units," which shoot the stunts as well as backgrounds that do not require the presence of the actors. In the James Bond movie *Tomorrow Never Dies*, for instance, this division of labor had five different people playing the James Bond character: Pierce Brosnan, the star, was playing James Bond at the Frogmore Studio outside of London, while four stuntmen at four different locations were playing him in stunts. Similarly, in *Charlie's Angels: Full Throttle*, the "Dylan" character, was played by Drew Barrymore and stuntwomen Heidi Moneymaker, a star gymnast, and Gloria O'Brien. (Lucy Liu's character had four stunt players.)

A second, and even more compelling reason, is the cast insurance requisites. Even if stars are physically present during the shooting of perilous stunts, the production's insurers prohibit them from substituting for the stuntmen. Since Harold Lloyd nearly lost two fingers performing his own stunts in 1920, cast insurance has been an absolute requisite for a Hollywood movie. If a star is deemed an essential element in a movie—as Liu, Diaz, and Barrymore are in *Charlie's Angels: Full Throttle*—and the star becomes disabled, the insurer must cover the resulting loss, which in the case of *Charlie's Angel: Full Throttle* was about $120 million. Before issuing such expensive policies, and no Hollywood movie could be made without one, insurers go to great lengths to make sure that actors do not take any risks that could lead to even a sprained ankle or pulled muscle. Their representatives analyze every shot in the script for potential risks and scrutinize the stars' prior behavior on and off the screen. Once the production starts, they also station hawk-eyed agents on the set to make sure that the stars are not put in harm's way. They might require, for example, that a star standing on a stationary car be held by two safety men (masked in blue spandex so they can be digitally deleted from the final movie). Even if a director or producer were willing to risk injuring a star, the insurer would not allow it. So stars, as much as they might enjoy performing their fantasies, cannot do dangerous stunts for movies.

For the most part, stars do not tell these tall tales of daredevils on television out of either personal dishonesty, vanity, or egoism. It is their job to play a character in publicity appearances, just as it is the job of studios to hype their movies. Nor do others in these Hollywood productions, even if they were not bound by contractual restrictions on disclosures, or "NDAs," have reason to demystify such off-screen fictionalizing. The subterfuge is part of the system by which studios, talent agencies, music publishers, licensees, and others create, maintain, and profitably exploit the stars' public personalities. The more interesting question: why entertainment journalists, instead of challenging these preposterous claims, act as the stars' smiling attendants on this organized flight from reality? The answer: deception is a cooperative enterprise. By suspending their disbelief, the entertainment journalists get the stars on their programs.

PART III
HOLLYWOOD'S INVISIBLE MONEY MACHINE

WHY *LARA CROFT: TOMB RAIDER* IS CONSIDERED A MASTERPIECE OF STUDIO FINANCING

A Hollywood studio has both an official budget, which is often leaked to trade papers such as *Variety* and *The Hollywood Reporter*, to show how much money it is supposedly costing to produce, and a closely-held production cost budget that shows how much money the movie is actually costing to produce. The latter budget, which is rarely seen by anyone outside of a studio, takes into account the money the studio gets from government subsidies, tax shelter deals, product placement, and other sources that greatly offset the amount of its own money that a studio actually has to sink into a film. A vice president at Paramount explained to me how these invisible maneuvers, including pre-sales abroad, can reduce the risk to practically zero. As an example, he cited Paramount's *Lara Croft: Tomb Raider* as a "minor masterpiece" in the arcane art of studio financing. Although the official budget for this 2001 production was $94 million and reported even higher in the press, the studio's outlay was only $8.7 million. How?

First, Paramount got $65 million from Intermedia Films in Germany in exchange for distribution rights to *Lara Croft: Tomb Raider* for six countries: Britain, France, Germany, Italy, Spain, and Japan. These "pre-sales" left Paramount with the rights to market its film to the rest of the world.

Second, it arranged to have part of the film shot in Britain so that it would qualify for Section 48 tax relief. This allowed it to make a sale-lease-back transaction with the British Lombard Bank through which (on paper only) *Lara Croft: Tomb Raider* was sold to British investors, who collected a multimillion subsidy from the British government, and then sold it back to Paramount via a lease and option for less than Paramount paid (in effect, giving it a share of the tax-relief subsidy). Through this financial alchemy in Britain, Paramount netted, up front, a cool $12 million. Third, Paramount sold the copyright through Herbert Kloiber's Tele Munchen Gruppe to a German tax shelter. Because German law did not require the movie to be shot in Germany, and the copyright transfer was only a temporary artifice, the money paid to Paramount in this complex transaction was truly, as the executive put it, "money-for-nothing." Through this maneuver, Paramount made another $10.2 million in Germany, which paid the salaries of star Angelina Jolie ($7.5 million) and the rest of the principal cast.

Before the cameras even started rolling, then, Paramount had earned, risk-free, $87 million. For arranging this financial legerdemain Paramount paid about $1.7 million in commissions and fees to middlemen, but that left it with over $85.3 million in the bank. So, its total out-of-pocket cost for the $94-million movie was only $8.7 million.

Since Paramount could be assured of selling the pay-tv rights to its sister company, Showtime, with which it had an output deal, for $8.5 million, it had little, if any, risk. As it turned out, the movie brought into Paramount's coffers over $100 million from theaters, DVDs, television, and other rights.

Of course, it's not only Paramount that employs these devices. Every studio uses them to minimize risk. In the case of the *Lord of the Rings* trilogy, New Line covered almost the entire cost by using a combination of German tax shelters, New Zealand subsidies, British subsidies, and pre-sales. The lesson here is that things in Hollywood— and especially numbers—are not what they appear to be, proving, yet again, that in Hollywood, the real art of movies is the art of the deal.

MONEY-FOR-NOTHING FROM GERMANY

A loophole in Germany's tax code provided a good portion of the studios' profits at least up until Germany attempted to close it in 2007. This "money for nothing," according to the vice presidents at Paramount responsible for arranging these deals, had been earning $70 million to $90 million annually. Best of all, there's no risk or cost for the studio (other than legal fees).

Here's how it works: Germany allows investors in German-owned film ventures to take an immediate tax deduction on their film investments, even if the film they're investing in has not yet gone into production. If a German wants to defer a tax bill to a more convenient time, a good way to do it is by investing in a future movie. The beauty of the German laws as far as Hollywood is concerned is that, unlike the tax laws in other countries, they don't require that films be shot locally or employ local personnel. German law simply requires that the film be produced by a German company that owns its copyright and shares in its future profits. This requisite presents no obstacle for studio lawyers.

The Hollywood studio starts by arranging on paper to sell the film's copyright to a German company. Then, they immediately lease the movie back—with an option to repurchase it later. At this point, a German company appears to own the movie. The Germans then sign a "production service agreement" and a "distribution service agreement" with the studio that limits their responsibility to token and temporary ownership.

For the privilege of fake ownership, the Germans pay the studio about 10 percent more than they'll eventually get back in lease and option payments. For the studio, that extra 10 percent is instant profit. If studio executives don't crow in public about such coups, it's probably out of fear that such publicity will induce governments to stiffen their rules—as, for example, Germany periodically attempts to do by amending its tax code. When you've got a golden goose, you don't want to kill it while it's still laying eggs.

HOW DOES A STUDIO MAKE A WINDFALL OUT OF BEING ON THE LOSING SIDE OF A JAPANESE FORMAT WAR?

Although rarely, if ever, discussed outside a corporate inner sanctum, studios make so-called replication output deals in which studios get paid large amounts from Japanese and other foreign manufacturers to support their formats. Consider, for example, Paramount and Dreamworks' win-win replication deal with Toshiba. In August 2007, in a last desperate effort to prevent its waning HD-DVD format from losing out to Sony's Blu-ray format, Toshiba offered Paramount and Dreamworks (which Paramount distributes) $150 million to put out the high-definition versions of their movies exclusively as HD-DVD. In such deals, the DVD manufacturer pays studios upfront cash for the right to make its DVDs. Supposedly, it is an advance that the manufacturer eventually gets back from selling the DVDs back to the studio's video division in much the same way a publisher earns back the advance it gives an author. In this case, Toshiba paid Paramount and Dreamworks a cool $150 million advance even though sales of HD-DVDs were so meager in 2007 that Toshiba was unlikely to ever earn back the entire advance. The wrinkle to the deal was that the studios, Paramount and Dreamworks, agreed not to continue releasing their movies in the rival Blu-ray format.

For Paramount, it was a particularly sweet deal because the payment was booked as a "reduction in cost of goods" for its Home Video division, which meant it did not have to allocate it to any of the titles released on DVD, or share it with writers, directors, stars, other participants, or even equity partners. Then came the real windfall: in March 2008, Toshiba abandoned the HDDVD format, so the studios got to keep almost all of the $150 million, and then re-released all their movies in the winning Blu-ray format.

Replication output deals go all the way back to the days of videos, when in 1981 Thomas McGrath, a Harvard MBA at Columbia, pioneered them. They rapidly became part of Hollywood's invisible money-making apparatus. Paramount, for example, made a quarter billion dollars from just three deals: $50 million dollars from Toshiba for agreeing to release *Titanic* on DVD in time for Christmas sales, $150 million from Panasonic for agreeing to allow them take over video replication from another manufacturer (Thompson), and $50 million from the law firm of Ziffrin, Brittenham and Circuit City stores for agreeing to support the DIVX format. Since the DIVX format was never launched, Paramount got to keep the money.

The $150 million Toshiba paid Paramount and Dreamworks not to release their titles on Blu-ray was a worthy continuation of this tradition. Such windfalls, even if not visible to the public, are what assure studios a true Hollywood Ending: bottom-line profits even when their films fail at the box office.

ROMANCING THE HEDGE FUNDS

Ever since Hollywood established its powerful hold over the global imagination, its studios have sought outside investors to help pay for their movies. The list of these "civilians" stretches from William Randolph Hearst, Joe Kennedy, and Howard Hughes in the 1920s to Edgar Bronfman, Sr., Mel Simon, Paul Allen, and Philip Anschutz in more recent times. Some such super-rich investors wanted to participate in the selection, casting, and production of the movies. (Hearst, Kennedy, and

Hughes, for example, all insisted that their mistresses be given choice roles.) Other civilians, such as the thousands of investors in Disney's Silver Screen partnerships, sought only the tax-sheltering benefits, but the IRS almost entirely eliminated this loophole by the early 1980s. And some civilians, including hedge funds, actually thought they could make money by negotiating more favorable deals with the studios.

But whatever motives such civilians may have for putting money in Hollywood movies, why do studios want outside funding? When I put the question to a thirty year veteran of studio corporate financing in December 2008, he shot back:

"No journalist who has ever written about movie financing has ever bothered to ask the question: why are the world's largest and most solvent media companies raising outside capital? Journalists all seem to buy, hook, line, sinker, and press release, the line that we [studios] need money." He noted that it was in a studio's interest to cry poverty, if only to get stars and their agents to reduce their demands for compensation, adding, "In my thirty years in this business I have never ceased to be amazed by this gullibility." Yes, studios can self-finance their entire slate of movies, and, unlike independent producers, they have sufficient revenues flowing from licensing of DVDs and TV rights to meet any film financing needs. The reason for recruiting outside financing is that the studios can make an "asymmetric deal" with an outsider, which means the outside investor gets a smaller share of the total earnings than does the studio on an equal investment of capital. And it is not only journalists who are gullible. Take JP Morgan Chase, which sent out a "teaser" to hedge funds, reading, "Despite compelling economic returns, major film studios are capital constrained and often must seek co-financing arrangements with other studios and other outside sources," and offered hedge funds "a unique opportunity to participate in the most profitable segment of the motion picture industry."

Hedge funds brimming with excess capital—at least up until the crash in 2008—made perfect civilian recruits for Hollywood, except that hedge fund managers had neither the expertise nor time to evaluate the prospects of individual films. In 2003, Isaac Palmer, then a young senior vice president at Paramount, came up with a brilliant solution. Studios could offer hedge funds a cut of their internal rate of return. This internal rate of return is not limited to so-called "current production," or the theatrical releases, on which studios almost always lose money. Rather, the rate subsumes every penny the studio makes from every source including pay-tv, DVDs, licensing to cable and network television, in-flight entertainment, foreign pre-sales, product placement, and toy licensing. So, even in a bad year, such as 2003, when Paramount released enough bombs to get the studio head fired, its internal rate of return was around 15 percent. This return also included the profits from the company's copyright lease-back sales to foreign tax shelters. (Palmer himself had structured one such deal that netted Paramount $130 million.) Plus, if the studio has a single big breakout movie, as it did in 1999–2000 with *Titanic*, the internal rate of return could leap to as high as 23 to 28 percent.

A safe 15 percent return, with a possible kicker in the event of a hit, proved very attractive to Wall Street. Palmer and his associates at Paramount worked out a deal with Merrill Lynch through which the hedge funds put up 18 percent of the capital for twenty-six consecutive Paramount movies in 2004 and 2005 through a vehicle called Melrose Investors, which then was extended through 2007. What makes this deal asymmetric is that Paramount also took a 10 percent distribution fee off the top on all the revenues, money which the hedge funds do not share. Since this cut comes from the gross, it makes Paramount, but not the hedge fund, a dollar-one gross player in its own movies.

Other studios had even sweeter or more asymmetric deals with hedge funds. Legendary Pictures, for example, was organized as a vehicle through which hedge funds, such as AIG Direct Investments and Bank of America Capital Investors, could sink a half-billion dollars into

Warner Bros. movies. But, unlike the Melrose Partners deal, the Legendary Pictures investors do not participate in the entire slate of Warner Bros. movies, which means that they do not really participate in the internal rate of return.

In its asymmetric deals with Wall Street studios enhance their own returns by getting a distribution fee on their investors' share of the revenues. And remain true to the Hollywood tradition of giving civilian investors the short end of the stick.

ENDING UP ON THE WRONG END OF THE DEAL

Back in 2003, after Kirk Kerkorian let it by know that he was (yet again) prepared to sell MGM, Viacom, which owns Paramount, considered buying it. Although MGM no longer had sound stages, backlots, or other physical facilities, and now produced only a handful of movies, it owned an incredibly valuable asset: a film library with 4,100 motion pictures and 10,600 television episodes. The crown jewels of this collection were its James Bond movies, possibly the most valuable entertainment franchise ever created. By licensing these titles over and over again to pay-tv, cable networks, and television stations around the world, this library brought in roughly $600 million a year. But that gross was an elusive number as it had to be split with others who had rights in the titles. Each title had its own contractual terms governing payments to partners, talent, guilds, and third parties. Just making these payments entailed issuing more than 15,000 checks per quarter. Not only did titles have different pay-out requisites, but their future revenue stream depended on factors specific to each movie, such as the age of its stars, its topicality, and its genre. To evaluate the library, Viacom assigned a team of fifty of its most experienced specialists to estimate how much each and every title would bring in over a decade. The Herculean job took the team two months. From this analysis, as well as considering other benefits of merging MGM with Paramount, Viacom's executives agreed MGM was worth between $3.5 and $4 billion. But before they could arrive at a bid price, Viacom's president, Mel Karmazin, asked his team whether the value of MGM's vast library would go the way of the music industry, which had been decimated by Internet downloading. When none of the executives could rule out that possibility, Karmazin said "In that case, we are not bidding on MGM." Disney, after a similar deconstruction of MGM's complex library, valued it at $3 billion, and also opted not to bid on the company.

Sony had a very different agenda for MGM. Since it had staked much of its corporate future on Blu-ray as a high-definition format, it needed to get other major studios to choose it over HD-DVD. Sony had learned from bitter past experience that format wars are often decided not by superior technology but by side payments made to studios. Toshiba and Microsoft (which had Xbox) were already offering huge cash inducements to put their titles exclusively on the HD-DVD format. Such pay-off competition could prove extremely expensive given the deep pockets of Toshiba and Microsoft, so Sony, which needed to establish Blu-ray for its PlayStation 3 as well as its movies, saw another route to victory. If it could put the huge library of MGM titles exclusively on Blu-ray, together with its own library and the Columbia Tristar library (which it also owned), Toshiba and Microsoft, no matter how many side payments they made, would not be able to establish their rival format. To this end, Sony did not need to itself spend billions to acquire MGM, it only had get effective control of MGM's library for a few years. So it put together a consortium that would be financed mainly by Wall Street private equity funds. And it would lead the consortium.

Even though the LBO would wind up costing $4.85 billion, Sony invested only $300 million of its own funds (and for that it got the profitable right to distribute MGM movies). Another $300 million came from the Comcast Corporation in return for the rights to put MGM's library on Pay Per View on its vast cable system. The rest of the equity money came from renowned Wall Street investors Providence Equity Partners, Texas Pacific Group, DLJ Merchant Banking Partners, and Steve Rattner's Quadrangle Group. These savvy funds put in a cool billion dollars. The leverage part of the deal was organized by JP Morgan Chase, which very profitably arranged, since it also got a fee, for the consortium to borrow $3.7 billion (or up to $4.2 billion, if needed) from some 200 banks. The deal closed in September 2004.

For Sony, the gambit succeeded brilliantly. Putting some 1,400 MGM titles exclusively on Blu-ray, helped established Blu-ray as the industry standard for high-definition, and it won the format war. It also made back a large share of its $300 million investment just on the distribution fee it earned on two new Bond movies, *Casino Royale* (2006) and *Quantum of Solace* (2008). But for the Wall Street players, it was nothing short of a disaster. To cut to the chase, they lost almost all their entire billion dollar investment. They had relied, perhaps naively, on impressive-looking projections showing that the net cash flow from the MGM movie and television library would be sufficient to pay the interest over a decade on the nearly $3.7 billion of debt. What they had not counted on was a sea change in DVD sales. In the US alone, MGM's net receipts from DVDs fell from $140 million in its 2007 fiscal year (which ended March 31, 2008) to just $30.4 million by

2010. As a result of collapsing sales, higher pay-out for participants, increased distribution costs and other distribution problems, MGM's crucial operating cash flow catastrophically fell from $418.4 million in 2007 to minus $54.2 million by 2010. In addition, it owed Fox Home Video $60 million for an "adjustment" in the DVD distribution contract it had taken over from Sony. By October 31, 2009 MGM, sinking in a sea of red ink, found itself unable to make its mandated interest payments on the $3.7 billion it owed banks.

Ordinarily when a company fails to make such payments, its bank creditors can seek to recover their money by forcing the company into bankruptcy. With MGM, however, the bankruptcy option presented a real problem since many of its intellectual property rights, including those to make sequels in the James Bond franchise, stipulate that in the event of bankruptcy they would automatically revert to another party. In the case of the James Bond franchise, for example. the sequel rights would revert to Danjaq, LLC. (These bankruptcy clauses are not mentioned, even in a footnote, in the 38-page "Confidential Information Memorandum" that MGM sent out to prospective buyers in the winter of 2009.) So the creditors, learning that bankruptcy would destroy a significant part of the remaining value of MGM, gave it a three month "forbearance," which meant it had until January 31, 2010 to come up with the money. The idea was that MGM would sell itself to a white knight and use the proceeds to repay the banks. The deal book was sent out to a dozen or so prospective buyers calling for bids by January 15. The replies, however, were disappointing, with none of the serious bids coming within $1.6 billion of what MGM owed its creditors. The hedge funds wrote down 85 percent of their billion dollar investment. The lesson here for Wall Street is that when a Hollywood deal seems too good to be true—it may not be.

Nevertheless, hedge funds provided enough fresh money for MGM to produce new installments in its James Bond franchise, and produce TV series. Can a zombie studio such as MGM be brought back to life? Amazon demonstrated that such feats are possible n the age streaming. In May 2021, it announced it was buying MGM for no less than $8.45 billion to boost its streaming ambitions by gaining control of its library of 4,000 films and 17,000 TV shows as well as its James Bond franchise. So another part of Hollywood was swallowed up by the insatiable appetite of a streamer.

**THE RISE OF THE HOME
ENTERTAINMENT ECONOMY**

Worldwide MPA Studio Receipts
(Inflation-corrected, 2007 US Dollars)
Billions of dollars

Year	Theatrical	Video / DVD	TV (including pay-tv, PPV)	Total	Theatrical as % of Total Revenue
1948	8.5	0	0	8.5	100
1980	4.9	2.2	4.1	9.22	55
1985	3.3	2.6	7.4	13.3	25
1990	6.8	6.5	10.1	22.4	22
1995	6.2	11.9	11.6	29.7	19.6
2000	6.5	13.1	15.5	35.1	19.4
2003	8.7	21.1	18.7	48.5	17.9
2004	8.1	22.8	18.1	49	16.9
2005	7	22.6	16.9	46.5	15.1
2006	8.2	19.8	16.1	44.1	18.5
2007 *	8.8	17.9	16.2	42.9	20.4

* The studios stopped furnishing these
revenue numbers to the MPA in 2008.

EVER WONDER WHY NEW YORK LOOKS LIKE TORONTO IN THE MOVIES?

In the golden era of the studio system, a studio mainly confined its principal photography to its own highly-efficient sound stages and back lots, where it could deploy its contract stars and technicians, and had whatever exotic material was necessary shot by a traveling second unit. Nowadays, movies are shot all over the world, but in scouting locations, producers are not seeking the most authentic settings or spectacular production values. The lure is government subsidies. As one producer put it, movies, like ladies of the night, go where the money is. Such subsidies can finance up to a large share of the below-the-line budget through a series of maneuvers in which a movie first qualifies for tax credits by employing local actors and technicians, then selling those credits.

Hence the appeal of Canada. The Canadian federal government provides foreign producers with a subsidy, called the Film Production Services Tax Credit, which in 2008 equaled 16 percent of Canadian labor costs. In addition, British Columbia offers an additional 18 percent rebate on labor from that province. Finally, there is a 20 percent break on digital effects, if they are done in Canada. In order to qualify for this tax credit—which the producer sells through a Canadian partner—either the director or the screenwriter and one of the two highest paid actors must be Canadian, which might partly explain the demand for Canadian actresses, such as Alex Johnson, the star of *Final Destination 3*.

Heeding the siren call of subsidies, Hollywood moved north over the last decade, outsourcing to Canada no fewer than 1,500 movies and television productions. Producers found Vancouver could double for middle America, Toronto could stand in for New York City (especially if the director avoids wide shots), and Calgary makes for a great American West. At times, some script adjustments were required to accommodate the cold reality of the North. For example, in *Final Destination* 3, which was filmed in British Columbia, the climactic attack was supposed to occur during an outdoor party on the Fourth of July but since it was not feasible to have actors wear summery clothes during Vancouver's chilly spring, the holiday was changed to the town's tricentennial celebration. But for Hollywood's illusion-makers, who have much experience in geographically deluding audiences, such adjustments are worthwhile, especially if they finance one third or so of the budget with a depressed currency, the plummeting Canadian loonie. As a result of this location shopping, Canada has emerged as a Hollywood stand-in for the United States.

THE FOREIGN MIRAGE

When Hollywood movies fail to find audiences in America, it is often claimed that these movies redeem their losses overseas. The assumption here is that the box office receipts abroad are pure gravy for the movie studios. For example, the usually financially-savvy *Wall Street Journal* reported on November 19, 2004, that three notable "duds" in America—*Troy, The Terminal*, and *King Arthur*—"ended up turning handsome profits" because "in each case, box office receipts from outside the US far outweighed domestic returns." It then cited impressive sounding numbers: *Troy* "made" $363 million internationally; *The Terminal*, $96.3 million internationally; and *King Arthur*, $149.8 million abroad—as if these receipts represented their salvation.

In reality, however, these impressive-sounding receipts represented the foreign theaters' revenue, not the studios' share of them. In fact, the studios get an even smaller share of the foreign than of the American box office. In 2007, the studios' share averaged about 40 percent of ticket sales. And from those revenues, studios have to pay for foreign advertising, prints, taxes, insurance, translations, etc. Once those expenses are deducted, the studios are lucky to wind up with 15 percent of what is reported as the foreign gross.

Consider, Disney's *Gone in 60 Seconds*. Its reported "foreign gross" was $129,477,395. Of that sum, Disney got $55,979.966, of which it paid out $37,986,053 in expenses.

They included:

Foreign Advertising	$25,197,723
Foreign Prints	$5,660,837
Foreign Taxes	$5,077,286
Foreign Versions	$822,997
Foreign Shipping	$454,973
Currency Conversion	$266,900
Foreign Trade Dues	$122,275

After paying these expenses, Disney was left with just $17,993,913—a far cry from the reported $129,477,395 "gross." And the film is still over $153 million in the red. So while the foreign box office helps, it does not necessarily make a movie profitable.

For Streamers, foreign money is not a mirage. Unlike Hollywood studios They do not have to worry about the cost of shipping, taxes, trade dues, prints or advertising or the split with foreign theaters of distributors. They simply earn an addition fee with each overseas subscriber they add.

PUSHING THE PSEUDO REALITY ENVELOPE

When the *Wall Street Journal* cited the on-screen brand choices of two movie stars, Steve Martin driving a Mercedes Benz S-Class sedan in *Shopgirl* and Matthew Broderick driving one in *The Stepford Wives*, as empirical evidence that this model of Mercedes has practically become an icon for corporate chieftains, movie stars, and diplomats, it showed how effective product placement can be in movies. It was not the movie stars themselves who drive that brand of car, but their fictional characters who are cast with those cars by the producers.

The casting of cars goes back to the 1974 James Bond film *The Man with the Golden Gun*, whose producer, Albert "Cubby" Broccoli, made a deal to use American Motors vehicles in all the chase scenes in exchange for advertising dollars to promote the movie. The function of such product placement is to subtly associate the car brand with a class of people. Hence the choice of Chrysler Jeeps in *Lara Croft Tomb Raider: The Cradle of Life*, Audis in *I, Robot* and *Transporter 2*, General

Motors cars in *The Matrix Reloaded,* and Ford cars on *X-Files* and *24.* Product placement now includes products ranging from Apple computers in *Mission: Impossible* to Nokia phones in *The Saint* to almost any brand mentioned on NBC's *The Apprentice.*

The persistence of a brand in a studio's movies often signifies nothing more than a package deal. The Weinstein Company, for example, entered into a multi-year marketing alliance with L'Oréal Paris, the world's largest "beauty" brand, which will result in the integration of L'Oréal's products in the Weinstein brothers' movies. And, with digital technology, even if a L'Oréal product was not shot in the movie itself, it can be inserted later (as is now being done with old TV series). One successful producer, whose movies have been distributed by the Weinstein brothers, noted "Product placement gigs will become a major source of production financing in the future, in which a movie provides a controlled world of good-looking stars wearing a certain brand of clothing for an hour and a half, in exchange for which the brand manufacturer pays for a large share of the production."

Product placement, though at a much smaller (and discrete) scale, has a long history in Hollywood. In the 1930s, De Beers, for example, had its agents give studio executives sample diamonds to use in roles that showed women being swayed by the gift of a diamond jewel. Not uncommonly, the diamonds were never returned. As brands took on more global significance, product placement became more open—and routine. Most product placements nowadays are barter deals. A manufacturer finances a cross-promotional ad campaign in return for their product being placed in a movie. In more recent James Bond movies, such as *Die Another Day* and *The World Is Not Enough*, for example, such ads for product placement deals were valued at over $30 million dollars. Cash deals are much rarer—and minuscule by comparison—but can prove useful in covering unforeseen contingencies. In *Terminator 3*, for example, the cash committed for product placements was used to guarantee the deferred part of Jonathan Mostow's $4,960,000 director's fee.

Not all product placement deals accrue to the profit of the production itself. In the case of *Natural Born Killers*, for example, a producer arranged for the director Oliver Stone and other members of the production to get two free pairs of cowboy boots in return for showing the boots' brand name, Abilene, on a truck passing by the open convertible driven by the character Mallory Knox (Juliette Lewis). This meant that the two vehicles—Mallory's car and the Abilene boot truck—coming from opposite directions, had to arrive in front of the camera at precisely the same time. Over and over again, both drivers, starting their approach a half mile apart, had to be continually cued with walkie-talkies as the camera, which was mounted on a crane, swooped down. So, to get his free boots, Stone had to shoot numerous retakes, which delayed a production running at $300,000 a day.

For smaller independent movies, the fees for product placement, whether cash or barter, are much less. The going rate for a single product inclusion in an independent movie usually ranges between $50,000–$250,000. According to one knowledgeable independent producer, the most that's gained from the placements is some free products, some cash for the production, and some shared advertisement placement, and that is usually conditioned on the product making the final cut and the film getting a US release. Even so, for productions on a tight budget, bartering airplane tickets, hotel rooms, and automobile leases for product placement slots can result in more money being available for the filming itself—or post-production work. Nor is there any reason that product placement should not be part of the pseudo-reality of a movie. All the Oscar ceremony blather about social reality notwithstanding, movies are fictive concoctions. What goes into that concoction—including stars chosen for their ability to pre-sell foreign markets, locations chosen to qualify for government subsidies, and brands chosen for their production placement value—doesn't alter its fictional status. The only problem comes when the illusion of a movie is confused with the reality of the consumer zeitgeist—which of course is the ultimate purpose of the product placer.

THE NEW CIVIL WAR AMONG THE STATES

Not willing to leave all the glamor of providing backdrops for Hollywood movies to Canadian interlopers, states are now competing against each other to lure studios with lucrative incentives to shoot movies in their bailiwick. The incentive usually takes the form of awarding state tax credits to a movie, which a studio can then sell to corporations or individuals able to use them to offset their taxes. Warner Bros. and Paramount's 2008 film *The Curious Case of Benjamin Button* is a case in point. The film had been budgeted at over $160 million because of expensive computer-generated special effects needed in postproduction to age and de-age the characters played by Brad Pitt and Cate Blanchett. The producers figured out that by filming it in Louisiana—for example, substituting the Gulf coast at Mandeville for the English Channel—they could qualify for the tax credit not only on the scenes actually shot in Louisiana but also for the special effects done in Los Angeles-as-Louisiana. They were also awarded a 15 percent tax credit for the entire budget of the film, including the money spent out of state on special effects and other postproduction work. As a result, the producers were able to cash in $27,117,737 from these tax credits, a windfall they would have missed had they shot the movie in Hollywood. Of course, this largesse proved costly to Louisiana. In 2006, it doled out $121 million in tax credits and, after it was discovered that producers might be paying counter-bribes to qualify, the Louisianan who oversaw the program, Mark Smith, pleaded guilty to taking $67,500 in bribes to inflate production budgets for film companies. Even so, in 2008, more than seventy films and TV productions qualified for tax credits in Louisiana.

By 2008, no fewer than forty states were offering some kind of incentive to lure movies. Most used the same form of tax credit as Louisiana, which is then "monetized" for the studios by specialized financial companies, such as Screen Capital International. A few states simply rebate a percentage of the budget to the studio. New Mexico, for example, gives a 25 percent production cost rebate. As far as studios are concerned, the more the merrier, and the more complex the better. The incentive war between the states is just another opportunity   for   enrichment.

THE RISE AND FALL OF OUTPUT DEALS

In Hollywood, like its movies, El Dorados are found and lost. Consider the once rich pay-channel output deals, which, as late as July 2008, Bob Weinstein, the co-chairman of the Weinstein Company, could describe as "the bedrock of the business . . . not one company in this business could survive and succeed without one."

These quasi-secret deals originated back in the early 1980s, when Viacom's Showtime was desperately competing with Time Inc.'s HBO for access to cable viewers. These were known in the industry as "The pay-tv Wars." In those years, when DVDs were no more than a distant gleam in the eyes of Japanese manufacturers and videos were rented but not sold to the public, studio movies on pay channels drove cable subscriptions, and to get those subscriptions cable operators would pay big money to the dominant pay-tv channel, which was HBO. In this battle to dominate cable distribution, a battle HBO won, the pay channels needed the exclusive rights to movies, and offered to buy studios' entire slate of movies for many years. Although this war was rarely, if ever, mentioned in the entertainment media, many of the executives who negotiated these early deals, including Frank Biondi, Jonathan Dolgen, and Thomas McGrath, went on to run Hollywood studios. The price that was paid per title was adjusted by a formula that adjusted the payout, which averaged about $12 million, according to its box office results. In 1985, however, after HBO wound up paying $30 million for *Ghostbusters* because of its huge box office numbers, it began capping the maximum pay out at $12.5 million per title. So did the other pay-tv channels. Even so, payment to studios averaged close to $10 million a title up until 2005. A studio with twenty-five movies a year in its output deal would collect a quarter billion dollars in the US alone. This was pure gold since, unlike the theatrical release, in which theaters keep half of the box office, and then distributors deduct print and advertising outlay from what remains, almost all the money from the output deal went directly into the studios' coffers. And by 2000, the six major studios, and their subsidiaries, were taking in $1.1 billion from pay-tv.

In the new millennium, however, the ascendancy of the DVD in the 2000s, and later iTunes and other digital downloads, gave viewers alternative ways of watching movies in high quality at home before they became available on cable. In addition, according to a top executive of HBO, new subscription growth was flattening, movies or no movies, with the near saturation of household growth. To hold their audience, and cash in on the DVD boom, pay channels increased their investment in original programming, such as the series *Sex and the City, The Sopranos*, and *The L Word*. As a result, as the studios' multiyear output deals expired, the pay-tv channels drove harder and harder bargains with studios and became far more selective about what they would buy. Instead of buying a studio's entire output, pay channels found they could fill a large part of their 24-hour a day schedule by simply replaying more frequently their own inventory of movies and original programs. By 2009, they were buying less than half the number of studio movies that they had bought in 2005 and paying half the price per title in these output deals.

One of the first casualties of this cutback was New Line Cinema, a mini-studio that Time Warner had acquired in 1996. Up until 2007, it had an output deal with HBO, another Time Warner subsidiary, that guaranteed it about $80 million for twelve movies. When Jeff Bewkes became chairman of Time Warner in 2008, he found that HBO did not need the New Line movies, and the $80 million was largely being used to finance distribution organizations that could be folded into Warner Brothers. So Bewkes ended the sweetheart output deal, closed New Line (as well as its Fine Line and Picturehouse divisions) and did not renew the contracts of New Line co-founders Bob Shaye and Michael Lynne.

Paramount had a similar problem in 2008 with its output deal with Showtime after the pay channel became part of CBS, Inc. in the split up of Viacom. Unwilling to renew the rich sweetheart contract it signed with Paramount when both companies were part of Viacom, Showtime left Paramount without any output deal.

Not only is the gold is gradually petering out of the El Dorado of output deals, but streamers, which produce their own content, have no need for them.

FOR WHOM DOES THE MOVIE
BUSINESS TOLL?

Along the metaphoric road to getting movies to the greater public, the studios act as the toll collector. The major studios collect this toll in the form of a distribution fee not only on the movies that they produce and finance but on other people's movies that they distribute. No matter how well or badly a movie fares at the box office, no matter how much money outside investors have sunk into it, the studio takes its cut from the gross emanating from the box office, the video store, and the television stations. Each of the six big studios, Warner Bros., Disney, Fox, Sony, Paramount, and Universal, has a wholly owned distribution arm that distributes titles that it finances, titles that its co-finances with partners, and titles produced and financed by outside production companies and so-called studio-less studios. The reason that these six studios dominate distribution is that the multiplex owners who book movies believe that they alone have the wherewithal not only to open a movie in 3,000 or more theaters on any given weekend but to create a national audience for it.

The studios are in this powerful position because they have accrued over the past three decades an enormous reservoir of intangible good will with the chains that own the multiplexes by granting them such favors as readjusting the terms of their poorly-performing movies, extending their payment period, carving out zones to avoid destructive competition between the multiplexes, and providing them with a constant diet of franchised movies, such as *Pirates of the Caribbean, Spider-Man*, and *Harry Potter*, that fill their theaters with popcorn consumers. In return, the chains have given these studios a large measure of effective control over the booking and staging of wide openings, for example, inserting teaser trailers months in advance of the opening so that they can more precisely coordinate the marketing campaign. So if outside producers and financiers want to play in this game of wide-opening movies, which is where the big grosses are found, they have little choice but to pay the studios' price of admission: the distribution fee.

The fee varies according to the strength of the players. Studios usually charge a 30 percent distribution fee on the films they themselves finance. In Hollywood accounting, each of its movies is set up as an independent off-the books company, and the 30 percent fee is treated as a cost paid to an outside entity, even though the distributor is also fully owned by the same studio. The result of this fictional division is that a film, after paying this enormous tariff, rarely shows a profit, even if the studio is making a profit from the distribution fee, and so the writers, directors, actors, and other participants in the profit rarely see anything but red ink on their semi-annual statements.

When it comes to films that are financed by other people's money, the distribution fee is the subject of often contentious negotiations. Most outsiders needing to reach a wide audience wind up paying about 18 percent. Since the actual cost of distributing a movie is 8 percent, a figure which includes the incremental cost of PR specialists, media buyers, customs clearance, transportation, and lawyers' time, the studio makes as pure profit 10 percent of the gross revenues of a film on which some other party financed and took all the risk. Stronger players often negotiate the fee down to 12 percent, but that still leaves the studio a 4 percent profit on their gross, and hedge funds, which co-invest in entire slates of studio films, pay only 10 percent, yielding still a 2 percent profit. There are also "a few gorillas," as a Paramount exec calls them, whose movies are so vital to studios, that they pay only 8 percent, the magic number at which the studio makes no profit.

But such nonprofit arrangements are the exception, numbering in 2008, according to the Paramount executive, only three: Steven Spielberg's deal with Universal, and Dreamworks Animation and Marvel Entertainment's deals with Paramount. Most of these studio distribution deals with outsiders yield substantial profits on Other People's Money. A top executive at Disney calculated, for example, that Disney made over $80 million in 2005 from outsiders (after deducting its actual costs of distribution). This skim, which goes to the bottom line, makes the six studios the biggest gross players in Hollywood.

Up until 2009, the six major studios could extract this skim because they were the only game in town when it came to distribution. But then streaming created an alternative.   Movies could be freely distributed over the Internet.   All the streamers needed was content to attract subscribers.   For the first few years they licensed it from thew studios, Then, beginning in 2013, they found they could produce it themselves. At the point, studio executives realized the bells   were   tolling   for   them.

PART IV
HOLLYWOOD POLITICS

N THE PICTURE

In November 2009, Oliver Stone literally put me in the picture. I was seated at an oval table under an eerie light in what purported to be the office of the Chairman of New York Federal Reserve Bank. As the meeting continued throughout the night, people around screamed about the "moral hazard" of saving a failing investment bank. At one point, there was even a call from the White House dooming the bank in question. The frenetic scene is no more than a consensual hallucination directed by Oliver Stone for the movie *Wall Street 2: Money Never Sleeps*. (A sequel to his 1987 *Wall Street*.) The magnificently wood paneled room is actually the executive conference room of an insurance company, MetLife, which is serving as a location for this part of the filming. The eerie glow comes from powerful lamps ingeniously suspended from helium balloons above us. The shouting is coming from actors Frank Langella, Eli Wallach, and Josh Brolin. Although I had only a bit part in this drama, it provided me with an opportunity to see how a Hollywood movie is made from the vantage point of the set.

The project was initiated in 2005 by Edward R. Pressman, the producer of the original *Wall Street*, after he saw the fictional villain of *Wall Street* Gordon Gekko (portrayed by Michael Douglas) on the cover of *Fortune*, accompanied by a headline about the return of greed to Wall Street. Pressman reasoned that if eighteen years after the movie, Gekko was still the media's icon for greed on Wall Street, a sequel was in order. He owned the rights for the sequel but sought to interest Twentieth Century Fox, which had distributed the original *Wall Street*. Getting a movie made in Hollywood when the hero is not a comic book character was not an easy task. Just getting a script that was acceptable to Fox took four years—and three different (and very expensive) writers. Even then Fox's approval was conditional on the stars and director, as are almost all movie deals. Pressman persuaded Michael Douglas to again play Gekko, a role for which he had won the Oscar in 1988, and Oliver Stone (who had dropped out of the project earlier) to direct. Fox then agreed to finance it. Part of the $67 million budget could be retrieved from New York State and New York City's tax credit programs (which effectively reimburse 35 percent of the production budget spent in New York).

The Federal Reserve scenes were filmed over a long weekend about midway in the eleven-week shooting schedule. Through the seemingly endless retakes in which actors repeat virtually the same lines while extras behind them—each of whom is called by a number rather than a name—move to the exact same "mark," or position, Stone gradually perfects the illusion. Between each take, the time on the grandfather clock in the office is reset to the exact time as it was at the start of the previous scene. The process is not unlike the never-ending day in *Groundhog Day*. But surrounding the illusion-in-the making is an envelope of reality. It is peopled by a small army of technicians, including make-up artists, hair stylists, script supervisors, technical advisors, continuity girls, stand-by carpenters, wranglers, costumers, sound boom men, camera operators, film loaders, set decorators, and electricians. They work ceaselessly, rushing onto the set between takes, to maintain and repair the illusion. One of the advantages of a top director such as Stone is that he can get the best of the below-the-line talent, in this case such Oscar nominees as Rodrigo Prieto, the Mexican-born director of photography, whose credits include *Frida, Brokeback Mountain*, and *Babel;* Kristi Zea, the production designer, whose credits include *Revolutionary Road, Goodfellas*, and *The Silence of the Lambs;* and Tod Maitland, the versatile sound technician who won an Oscar for *Seabiscuit*.

Stone himself is constantly moving around the set, viewing scenes from different angles and talking to the actors and extras, often in whispers. At other times, he confers with technical advisors, including two former SEC lawyers who had actually attended the Fed meetings, asking them about such details as how coffee cups would be placed on the table or how precisely a phone call from the White House would be answered. When any unexpected difficulties arise, such as when the camera dolly creaks audibly on its tracks, he jokes with the cast, having a gift for putting actors at ease. But even with the amicable atmosphere, he has to keep the movie running on a tight schedule. Just the below-the-line expenditures for *Wall Street 2*, which does not include the compensation for the stars, writers, producers, or the director, is running about $220,000 a day for interior scenes (exterior and crowd scenes can be much more expensive). So unless he shoots the planned number of script pages a day, he will run over budget. While Hollywood players are often depicted in the media as profligate spenders, the opposite is true when it comes to studio executives supervising a movie that they are financing. Before *Wall Street 2* went into production, Fox went through the budget line by line, squeezing every penny it could out of the budget, even attempting to reduce the fees of major actors (all of whom have a "quote," or established price per movie). If the shooting ran over budget, Fox could ask that scenes be cut out of the script to get it back on track or use money from the post-production budget, which includes putting in visual effects (which are crucial in *Wall Street 2* since some scenes are shot with blank backgrounds), adding sound, and editing. So Stone manages to

adhere to the schedule, even when it requires him—
and his assistant directors—working grueling
fourteen hour days (as in the Federal Reserve Bank
scenes). And, as it turns out, he completes the
movie within a day of the targeted end of shooting.

When I arrive at the wrap party at the club Spin,
the cast, crew, and friends are huddled around
plasma TV screens, watching clips from the movie.
For most of them, it is their first opportunity to see
how Stone actually realized the scenes they had
worked in or on. As they watch, visibly impressed,
they often cheer with the sort of gusto one might
expect at a Super Bowl party when a touchdown is
scored. Everyone embraces Stone, the hero of the
evening, as he passes through the room. The club is
owned by Susan Sarandon (who had acted in the
movie) and features ping pong tables where Josh
Brolin and Mel Gibson (who was not in the movie)
engaged in a wild game. The celebration continued
into the early hours of the morning.

Unlike independent movies, which usually take
years to reach the theaters, studio movies have a
built-in release date from the moment they are
green-lighted. *Wall Street 2* opened at multiplexes
across America on September 24, 2010. And during
production Fox was already working on the
advertising and marketing campaign, which
required a huge investment in ads on cable and
network TV. The worldwide P&A budget probably
exceeded $40 million, which brought Fox's total

outlay to about $100 million. The original *Wall Street* did far better in earning critical acclaim and buzz than money. Fox's share of the American box office was only $20.2 million—and it fared far worse in foreign markets. The problem Fox had then, and faces again, is that movies that involve complex issues, such as a financial crisis on Wall Street, did not draw the teen-age audience conditioned to expect the fast tempo of the studio's superheroes. The $100 million gamble for Fox is that in the post-summer period, when the herds of teens are in school, it will be able to find an adult audience for the multiplexes.

PARANOIA FOR FUN AND PROFIT: THE SAGA OF *FAHRENHEIT 9/11*

Michael Moore had a problem in April 2004. He'd finished making *Fahrenheit 9/11* but had no American distributor. Mel Gibson's Icon Productions rejected the project back in April 2003. (Moore claims he had a signed contract before Gibson acquiesced to White House pressure. Icon executives deny any such contract existed.) Moore then went to Harvey Weinstein at Miramax, which since 1993 had been a wholly owned Disney subsidiary. Weinstein agreed to back the movie and signed a contract with Moore to acquire the rights. But in order to distribute the movie, Weinstein still needed the approval of his superiors at Disney because Weinstein's contract explicitly prohibited Miramax, a wholly owned subsidiary of Disney, from distributing any film that was vetoed by the Disney CEO. When then-CEO Michael Eisner exercised his veto in May 2003, Miramax, though it still held the rights to the film, could not distribute *Fahrenheit 9/11*.

By the time Eisner told Weinstein of his decision, the Miramax head had already given Moore $6 million from Miramax's loan account. Weinstein agreed that this advance was to be "bridge financing" that he would recover when he sold off the film's distribution rights. To make sure there was no misunderstanding, Disney's senior executive vice president Peter Murphy, who was also at the meeting, wrote Weinstein a letter on May 12, 2003, affirming that this money was "bridge financing" and that Weinstein had agreed to dispose of Miramax's interest in the film. For Moore, this $6 million in "bridge financing" was more than enough to make *Fahrenheit 9/11*. He acquired most of the footage from television film libraries at little, if any, cost and did not pay any of the on-camera talent (except for himself). On April 13, 2004, after Weinstein saw a rough cut, he went back to Eisner and asked him to reconsider his year-old decision not to distribute *Fahrenheit 9/11*. After getting a report on the content, which included footage from such sources as Al Jazeera and Al-Arabiya television, Eisner saw no reason to change his position. He again declared that Disney wouldn't have anything to do with the movie.

With the presidential election heating up, Moore needed to get his movie into theaters. Although Weinstein had told Eisner and Murphy that he planned to sell the film's distribution rights after it was screened at the Cannes Film Festival, Moore had a more expedient stratagem. On the *Fahrenheit 9/11* DVD, Moore says he resolved to get the film seen in America "by hook or by crook." His hook was censorship.

On May 5, 2004, the *New York Times* ran a front-page article headlined "Disney Is Blocking Distribution of Film That Criticizes Bush." The story included the sensational charge that Eisner "expressed particular concern that [choosing to distribute *Fahrenheit 9/11*] would endanger tax breaks Disney receives for its theme park, hotels, and other ventures in Florida, where Mr. Bush's brother, Jeb, is governor." The source for this allegation was Moore's agent, Ari Emanuel. Two days later, Moore claimed on his Web site that Disney's board of directors rejected *Fahrenheit 9/11* "last week." In fact, the Disney board had not made such a decision in 2004; the project had been vetoed in 2003.

Moore's excursion from reality proved a boon at Cannes. On May 22, 2004, the Cannes jury defied putative efforts to censor Moore by awarding *Fahrenheit 9/11* the prestigious Palme d'Or. Moore now had a golden palm in his hand and the media at his feet. With more free publicity than any Hollywood studio could afford to buy, *Fahrenheit 9/11* now stood to rake in a fortune. And Disney, which still controlled the movie's rights through its subsidiary Miramax, now got to decide who was going to profit from it. Disney had some experience dealing with Miramax's hot potatoes. Rather than distributing the controversial *Kids* and *Dogma*, Disney allowed Miramax founders Harvey and Bob Weinstein to buy the films back and set up short-lived companies to distribute them. But those potatoes were as small as they were hot. In the case of *Fahrenheit 9/11*, Eisner wasn't about to let the windfall escape into the Weinstein brothers' pockets.

Nor could Disney take the PR hit that would result from backtracking and distributing the movie itself.

Eisner's solution: Generate the illusion of outside distribution while orchestrating a deal that allowed Disney to reap most of the profits. Here's how the dazzling deal worked. On paper, the Weinstein brothers bought the rights to *Fahrenheit 9/11* from Miramax. The Weinsteins then transferred the rights to a Disney corporate front called Fellowship Adventure Group. In turn, that company outsourced the documentary's theatrical distribution rights (principally to Lions Gate Films, IFC Films, and Alliance Atlantis Vivafilms) and video distribution rights (to Columbia Tristar Home Entertainment).

Because of the buzz now attached to *Fahrenheit 9/11*, Harvey Weinstein extracted extremely favorable terms from these distributors, about one-third of what distributors typically charge. Their cut amounted to slightly more than 12 percent of the total they collected from the theaters. As a result, *Fahrenheit 9/11's* net receipts, what remains after the distributors deduct their percentage and their out-of-pocket expenses (mounting an ad campaign, making prints, dubbing the film), would be much higher than those of a typical Hollywood film.

Fahrenheit 9/11, now an event, took in more than $228 million in ticket sales worldwide, a record for a documentary, and sold 3 million DVDs, which brought in another $30 million in royalties. After the theaters took their share of the movie's gross (roughly 50 percent) and distributors deducted the marketing expenses (including prints, advertising, dubbing, and custom clearance) and took their own cut, the net receipts returned to Disney were $78 million.

Disney now had to pay Michael Moore's profit participation. Under normal circumstances, such documentaries rarely, if ever, make profits (especially if distributors charge the usual 33 percent fee). So, when Miramax made the deal for *Fahrenheit 9/11*, it allowed Moore a generous profit participation—which turned out to be 27 percent of the film's net receipts. Disney, in honoring this deal, paid Moore a stunning $21 million. Moore never disclosed the amount of his profit participation. When asked about it, the proletarian Moore joked to reporters on a conference call, "I don't read the contracts."

What of Disney? After repaying itself $11 million for acquisition costs, it booked a $46 million net profit, which Eisner split between two subsidiaries, the Disney Foundation and Miramax.

With his $21 million, Michael Moore had perhaps the happiest ending of all.

THE SAGA CONTINUES

While Disney made a profit on the paranoia in *Fahrenheit 9/11*, it led Eisner and other Disney executives to question whether Harvey Weinstein was worth the trouble he had caused the corporation. While Weinstein told journalists how much money he had made for Disney, an internal audit showed that Miramax under Weinstein, rather than adding to Disney's profits, actually was hemorrhaging rivers of red ink. This reversal of fortune proceeded from a loophole in the original deal that Jeffrey Katzenberg, then Disney's studio head, negotiated with Weinstein in 1993. The Weinsteins had demonstrated a superb gift for finding, shaping, and marketing independent films like *Sex, Lies, and Videotape* and *The Crying Game*. To give the brothers a powerful incentive to ferret out similar arty winners, Disney agreed to give them a performance bonus of between 30 percent and 35 percent of their film profits, a bonus that would be calculated each fiscal year. The deal also tied Miramax's capital budget for acquiring and producing films to its annual performance. So, the more money Miramax made in a fiscal year, the more money the Weinsteins made and the bigger the capital budget of their Miramax division. The loophole was that Disney agreed to calculate Miramax's profits in a fiscal year solely on the films released that year. In making what seemed like a minor concession to Weinstein so that he could use his discretion in timing the marketing of art films, Disney did not foresee how brilliantly he would game the calendar to create the illusion of profits for Miramax and the reality of huge bonus payments for himself and his brother, Bob. He simply shifted potential money-losing films into future fiscal years so that they didn't reduce either his bonus or Miramax's capital budget. To prevent Weinstein from overspending, Eisner later imposed a further condition on the deal: For every dollar Miramax exceeded its capital budget, a similar amount was deducted from the Weinsteins' annual bonus. To avoid this penalty, Weinstein could delay releasing high-budget films in years in which he was close to exceeding his capital budget. As a result, even more films got dumped into Weinstein's limbo of unreleased movies. For example, Zhang Yimou's *Hero*, which had been acquired at Sundance in 2002, was held for more than two years so that its nearly $20 million cost would not count against the Weinsteins' bonus. *Hero* was released in 2004, a year less profitable for Miramax in which no bonus would be paid anyway.

In 2005, Eisner decided not to renew the Weinsteins' contract. Whereas Miramax belonged lock, stock, and barrel to Disney, the Weinstein brothers had a claim to subsidiary Dimension Films, which Eisner wanted to keep at Disney. So he had to negotiate an exit package for the Weinsteins. Enter Hollywood lawyer (and Shakespearean scholar) Bertram Fields, who got them a $130 million settlement (partially based on what turned out to be Miramax's phantom profits in prior fiscal years) and allowing Harvey and Bob Weinstein to create a new film company, The Weinstein Company.

After their departure, Disney released many of the delayed movies, which produced losses in 2005 alone of over $100 million. Harvey Weinstein, known for his artful films, also demonstrated with Disney that he had mastered the artful steal that amazed even Hollywood. Weinstein's career ended badly. In February 2020, he was convicted of rape and sexual assault in New York and sentenced to 23 years   in   prison.

PLUS ÇA CHANGE: PARAMOUNT'S REGIME CHANGE

The principal asset of a modern studio nowadays, aside from its library of movie titles and other intellectual properties, is its human capital, which includes executives with the negotiating skills, judgment, charm, and goodwill within the industry to get top stars, make favorable production deals, and profitably organize the release of movies. In the spring of 2004, following a string of six box office flops in 2003, Sumner Redstone, the chairman of Paramount's parent company, decided Paramount needed a new infusion of human capital. In the regime change, Jonathan Dolgen and Sherry Lansing, who had run the studio for the past decade, were out. Brad Grey, a dynamic forty-seven-year-old television producer and talent manager, would replace them. Even though he had no previous experience in running a movie studio, Redstone gave him a mandate to turn the studio around.

But turnaround from what? Despite its flops, the Dolgen-Lansing decade was hardly a disastrous one. During that period, 1994–2004, Paramount released six out of its ten highest grossing films in history, including *Titanic*, and in eight out of their ten years their division (which included television as well movies) scored record profits. They set up lucrative co-production deals with Dreamworks SKG, established the *Mission Impossible* franchise with Tom Cruise, and created three profitable distribution labels—MTV Films, Nickelodeon Films, and Paramount Classics. Dolgen's skill was the art of the deal which reduced Paramount's risk by using Other People's Money, his specialty being off-balance sheet financing and foreign subsidies to pay for a large part of a film's production costs. Through them, Dolgen and Lansing managed to achieve an average return on invested capital of nearly 60 percent during their ten years. Even in their worst year, 2003, they hit their targeted profit numbers.

Enter Brad Grey. He wasted little time in dismantling the team that his predecessors had built. Within six months, almost every senior executive "ankled," as *Variety* colorfully describes exiting a studio, including Rob Friedman, the head of worldwide distribution and marketing; Thomas Lesinski, the president of the Home Video division; Donald DeLine, the head of film production; Jack Waterman, the president of pay-tv; Gary Marenzi, the head of international TV; and Tom McGrath, the architect of the studio's off-balance sheet financing strategy. In all, over 100 executives were either fired or left Paramount in the regime change. "Even by the harsh standards of Hollywood such wholesale bloodletting is unprecedented," one former Paramount executive said in an email.

Gray also cancelled most, if not all, of the movie projects in process in 2005. Letting it be known that Paramount would place less emphasis, as part of the regime change, on deal-driven movies, he cancelled five such projects based on German and Spanish tax deals, which would have produced about $50 million in bottom line profits. (The financial vice president working on these deals, getting the message, promptly resigned.) But replacing such projects, and packaging scripts with stars, directors, and financing, takes many months, if not years. And by the fall of 2005, Paramount still did not have enough viable projects in the pipeline to provide the studio's distribution arm with product for 2006 and 2007. The solution Grey found was for Redstone to buy Dreamworks SKG for $1.6 billion.

To finance this deal, Redstone sold Dreamworks' movie library to hedge funds for $900 million. As a result, Paramount got thirty-odd Dreamworks projects— including *Dreamgirls* and *Transformers*—to replace the Dolgen-Lansing development projects.

The new regime, at Redstone's prodding, also ended its deal with Cruise-Wagner Productions, which had produced not only its *Mission: Impossible* franchise but its other tentpole film, *War of the Worlds*. The decision to end Cruise's contract, despite Redstone's PR jibes at Cruise, was, to quote *The Godfather*, "Not personal, Sonny; it's strictly business." The real problem was the rich split Cruise had negotiated with Paramount—22 percent of the gross revenues received by the studio on the theatrical release and the television licensing and a 12 percent cut of Paramount's total DVD receipts.

While Paramount was busy subsuming (and becoming) Dreamworks, the human capital at Dreamworks, including Steven Spielberg and his creative team, exited Paramount to create a new studio, backed by $500 million in Indian financing, which would be the new Dreamworks—or at least the sequel. Plus Ça Change or, as they say in Hollywood, that's show business.

TOM CRUISE, INC.

The gawkerization of Hollywood, entertaining as it may be to the public, blots out much of the reality underlying the movie business. Witness, for example, the treatment of Tom Cruise after *People* asked on its Web site in May 2005, if his relationship with the actress Katie Holmes represented "1. TRUE ROMANCE" or "2. PUBLICITY STUNT." In this pseudo-poll, in which subscribers with AOL's instant messaging could "vote" as many times as they wanted (paying a charge each vote), 62 percent of an unknown number of respondents chose "publicity stunt."

Once this statistically meaningless result was sent out on the PR wire, it spawned a frenzy of stories dangling the bizarre idea that the romance had been faked to publicize, in Cruise's case, Paramount's *War of the Worlds* and, in Holmes' case, Warner Bros.' *Batman Begins*. Frank Rich proclaimed in the *New York Times* that the affair was nothing more than "a lavishly produced freak show, designed to play out in real time," and that "the Cruise Holmes romance is proving less credible to Americans in 2005 than a Martian invasion did to those of 1938." As it turned out, Cruise and Holmes were subsequently engaged, married, and had a child.

What is entirely lost in the fog of media gossip, however, is the entrepreneurial role that Tom Cruise has carved out for himself in the New Hollywood. Consider, for example, the *Mission: Impossible* franchise. When Paramount decided to reinvent its TV series *Mission: Impossible* as a movie, Cruise not only starred in it, but he (along with producer partner Paula Wagner) produced it. In return for deferring his salary, he negotiated a deal for himself almost without parallel in Hollywood. To begin with, he got 22 percent of the gross revenues received by the studio on the theatrical release and the television licensing. The more radical part of the deal involved the video earnings (the deal was negotiated before DVDs replaced video tapes). When videotapes became a cash cow for Hollywood in the 1970s, each studio employed a royalty system in which one of its divisions, the home-entertainment arm, would collect the total receipts from them and pay another one of its divisions, the movie studio, a 20 percent royalty. This royalty became the "gross" number that the studios reported to their partners and participants. The justification for this system was that, unlike other rights, such as television licenses, which require virtually no sales expenses, videos have to be manufactured, packaged, warehoused, distributed, and marketed. So, the home-entertainment arm keeps 80 percent of the proceeds to pay these costs. The stars, directors, writers, investors, actors, guilds, pension funds, and other gross participants get their share of just the 20 percent royalty. If a star were entitled to 10 percent of the video gross, he or she would get 10 percent of the royalty, which, under this system, is only 2 percent of the real gross.

But not Cruise. He insisted on—and received—"100 percent accounting," which means that the studio, after deducting the out-of-pocket manufacturing and distribution expenses, paid Cruise his 22 percent share of the total receipts. As a result, Cruise earned more than $70 million on *Mission: Impossible,* and he opened the door for stars to become full partners with the studio in the so-called back end.

By 2000, the profits from DVDs had begun to alter Hollywood's profit landscape, and since it was now too complicated to track all the expenses, Cruise revised the deal with Paramount for the sequel *Mission: Impossible 2*. His cut of the gross was increased to 30 percent, and, for purposes of calculating his share of the DVDs, the royalty was doubled to 40 percent. So, he would get 12 percent of the total video/DVD receipts with no expenses deducted by Paramount. In return for this amazing deal, Cruise agreed to pay the only other gross participant, the director John Woo, out of his share.

As with *Mission: Impossible*, Cruise's company produced the film, and Cruise, who proved to be a relentlessly focused producer, brought *Mission: Impossible 2* in on budget. The movie went on to be an even bigger success than the original, earning more than a half-billion dollars at the box office and selling over 20 million DVDs. Cruise's share amounted to $92 million—and he was now the key element in Paramount's most profitable franchise. In light of such a success, Paramount initially agreed on the same deal with Cruise for *Mission: Impossible 3*. Even with Cruise's rich cut, Paramount would make money. According to an internal analysis by Paramount, each DVD, which retails for about $15 wholesale, costs the company only $4.10 to manufacture, distribute, and market.

Another 45 cents goes for residuals payments to the guilds, unions, and pension plans, leaving the studio with slightly over $10. So, even after giving Cruise his cut of $1.80 per DVD, Paramount stood to make more than $8 per DVD.

By 2004, DVDs were bringing into the studios' coffers more than twice as much money as the theatrical release of movies, and there was every reason to assume that *Mission: Impossible 3* would sell more DVDs than its predecessor. The budget, however, had increased to $180 million, so new Paramount studio chief, Brad Grey, asked for a renegotiation. After the dust had cleared, Cruise still had his huge percentage of the gross—it actually had improved since there were now no other gross participants. When released in 2006, the movie took in $397.8 million at the box office (nearly 70 percent of which came from foreign theaters)— which was less than the prior sequel— but Cruise's real profit came in his huge 12 percent cut of DVD sales. As it turned out, Cruise was now making much more from the franchise than Paramount, a disparity that so infuriated Paramount owner Sumner Redstone that he terminated Cruise's contract with Paramount in August 2006.

But Cruise did not go unemployed. MGM hired him in November 2006 to revive United Artists, a studio originally created in 1916 by such legendary Hollywood stars as Charlie Chaplin, Mary Pickford, and Douglas Fairbanks, Jr. but which had been dormant for twenty years. Merrill Lynch organized a $500 million line of credit to finance this enterprise. Whether or not Cruise can relaunch a moribund studio remains to be seen, but Cruise, as one of the handful of producers—along with George Lucas, Steven Spielberg, and Jerry Bruckheimer—who can reliably deliver a billion-dollar franchise, may yet succeed.

THE STUDIOS—REQUIRED READING

"People of the same trade seldom meet together, even for merriment and diversion, but the conversation ends in a conspiracy against the public, or in some contrivance to raise prices."
   —Adam Smith, *The Wealth Of Nations*

In Hollywood, thanks to the services of a secretive research firm called NRG, rival studio executives do not need to meet together and conspire. NRG helps them coordinate openings in such a way that their movies do not compete head-to-head for the same demographic slice of the audience. Founded in 1978 as the National Research Group, NRG— now a part of Nielsen Entertainment—supplies the same weekly "Competitive Positioning" report to each of the six major studios. NRG's founder, Joseph Farrell, signed all of the studios to exclusive contracts, ensuring that the data from his telephone tracking polls became the accepted standard. Because of this monopoly of information, the report provides the studios with a common basis on which to make their scheduling decisions.

Here is how the research is compiled. The NRG telephone pollsters ask a sample of likely moviegoers first whether they are "aware" of a specific movie and, if so, what is the likelihood that they will see it when it opens. They also ask the age and gender of the respondents. The NRG analysts break down the data from these tracking polls into four basic groups, or "quadrants": males under twenty-five, males over twenty-five, females under twenty-five, and females over twenty-five. (In some cases, the respondents are also divided by race.) From these results, NRG projects how well upcoming movies will do against each other in each audience quadrant should they open on the same weekend. For studios, the Competitive Positioning report is critical reading. Why? Nowadays, Hollywood has to create an audience for each and every movie via ad campaigns, appropriately called "drives" (as in "cattle drive"). "If we release twenty-eight films, we need to create twenty-eight different audiences," a Sony marketing executive lamented to me. Audience creation is a hugely expensive exercise. For a drive to work, it must not only round up a herd of moviegoers who favor the movie, it must also get this herd to move at a specific time: opening weekend.

This feat almost invariably requires buying a slew of ads on the limited number of television and cable series that the prospective herd grazes on during the week preceding the opening. To make sure they get the herd's attention, the ads are usually repeated eight times, which is why these drives cost so much. The multimillion-dollar drive runs into a serious problem, however, if a rival studio goes after the same herd that same week— for example, under-twenty-five males—by also buying a parcel of ads on the same shows. The herd then might be cross-pressured and confused, and certainly divided. Such a competition would likely spell failure for both rivals, since even the winner stands to lose a part of the audience to the rival film. To win, then, studios must avoid such conflicts, even if it means yielding to each other.

Enter NRG. The major studios can and do avert such titanic disasters by consulting the NRG Competitive Positioning report. Each studio gets an early warning from the NRG report when one of its films is on a collision course with a competitor's film that appeals to the same herd. By comparing the projected turnouts for both films in the crucial quadrant(s), the studios know which film will lose the matchup, and the losing studio can reschedule its opening to a different weekend, even if it's a less advantageous time period (i.e., not the summer and not the holidays).

Consider how Paramount captured the highly prized Fourth of July weekend in 2005 for *War of the Worlds* even though Warner Bros. had a major contender in *Batman Begins* and 20th Century Fox had *Fantastic Four*. In the NRG tracking polls, all three films did well with males under twenty-five (aka teens), the audience quadrant that's easiest to find clustered around TV programs and, hence, the easiest to stampede toward a July 4 weekend opening. But *War of the Worlds* was also strong in the under-twenty-five female quadrant, so it would easily best both *Batman Begins* and *Fantastic Four*. (In fact, it led in all quadrants.)

Warner Bros. averted a head-to-head competition by opening *Batman Begins* in mid-June, and 20th Century Fox opened *Fantastic Four* on the weekend following July 4. As a result, all three films won their weekend box office and could advertise themselves, as *Fantastic Four* did, as "America's No. 1 hit." No Adam Smith-type conspiratorial meetings were necessary between the rival studio executives of Paramount, Warner Bros., and 20th Century Fox in order to advantageously stagger their film openings so they did not collide. Of course, the weaker contender might try to bluff his way through. For example, in 2002, Disney's subsidiary Miramax had a direct conflict with Dreamworks SKG concerning the openings of their two competing films *Gangs of New York* and *Catch Me If You Can*, both starring Leonardo DiCaprio and both scheduled to open on December 25. Even though the Miramax film had a slightly higher "awareness" level in the targeted males-over-twenty-five audience, Dreamworks refused to yield. At that point, Harvey Weinstein, the president of Miramax, and Jeffrey Katzenberg, a founding partner of Dreamworks SKG, had breakfast in New York to discuss their movies' release dates. As Katzenberg later explained in an interview with the *New York Times:* "He [Weinstein] and I had many conversations about why releasing the movies on the same day was in none of our interest . . . as both companies have a big investment in Leo DiCaprio." A few days later, Miramax blinked by moving *Gangs of New York* to a different, and less favorable, opening date.

To be sure, NRG's services to the studios go well beyond helping studios avert unpleasant fender benders. It also analyzes much larger issues for the studios, essentially helping them to rethink their entire business models by examining the movies' declining share of the public's "wallet" and "clock" as they compete with music, DVDs, cable TV, downloading, and other forms of home entertainment. But without its Competitive Positioning reports studios would have a much harder time avoiding box office collisions.

AN EXPERT WITNESS IN WONDERLAND

In 2005, I became an expert witness in a Hollywood lawsuit that in nearly five years managed to consume over $20 million in legal fees. The heart of this Dickensian litigation was a contract between an author and producer for the making of *Sahara*, a $130 million action movie released in 2005 that starred Penelope Cruz and Matthew McConaughey and was directed by Breck Eisner (the son of ex-Disney chairman Michael Eisner). The plaintiff was the author Clive Cussler, who had sold the film rights to his 1992 bestselling book *Sahara* for $10 million and charged in his suit that his right to approve the final script had not been honored. He was represented in this suit by Hollywood lawyer Bertram Fields, who, according to his legend, had never lost a case (which is less impressive than it sounds because most Hollywood cases are settled out of court and the results are sealed). The defendant was Crusader Entertainment, a production company owned by oil tycoon Philip Anschutz, who, aside from his media properties, owned the majority stake in Regal Entertainment, America's largest movie theater chain. Anschutz, who was listed by *Forbes* as the thirty-sixth richest man in America with $8 billion in assets, was represented by O'Melveny & Myers, a legal powerhouse, which according to *American Lawyer*, had the top-rated litigation department in the country. The two law firms were located almost directly across the street from one another on the Avenue of the Stars in Century City, which once was the back lot of 20th Century Fox.

O'Melveny & Myers star litigator Alan Rader, who co-managed the *Sahara* case, retained me as an expert witness in 2005. He said that he had read my writings on the logic of Hollywood and wanted me to objectively lay out for the jury, possibly in a PowerPoint presentation, the economic reality behind the movie business. To prepare, I had to review a vast array of contracts, distribution deals, financial analyses, and other paperwork that might help me explain the requisites of the movie business. I also had to provide a lengthy deposition in Bert Fields' offices. Then, after years of convoluted maneuvering, the case actually went to trial, a rarity in Hollywood law. Six weeks later, the jury provided a surprise ending to the drama: Bert Fields, the man who putatively never lost a case, lost big for his client. Clive Cussler was ordered not only to pay Anschutz's company $5 million for undermining the success of the movie, but he had to pay him a staggering $13.9 million to cover his legal costs. In addition to this $18.9 million, Cussler also had to pay his own legal bill to Bert Fields, which presumably was also sizable.

But there was yet another twist: an appeal led to a judge nullifying the verdict in 2010 so that, in the end, the only winners were the lawyers who earned big fees.

Leaving aside the brilliant lawyering on both sides, the material I reviewed provided me with a key insight into how Hollywood works: the movie-business is a fee driven business. When viewed from the outside, movies, which are almost always set up as separate off-the-books entities, rarely, if ever, show a profit. Nevertheless, when viewed from the inside, they serve as vessels for collecting and dispensing billions of dollars in fees. In 2008, the fees from studio movies alone exceeded $8 billion. And these fees support a large part of the Hollywood community, including directors, stars, producers, and screenwriters, as well as the talent agents, business managers, and lawyers who represent them. But most of these fees are paid only if the production is approved, or green-lit, by a studio willing to finance it. So the big players in Hollywood, and their representatives, have a powerful incentive to use whatever means at their disposal to pressure studio executives into green-lighting their projects. For their part, studios also get a rich fee, the distribution fee, which allows them to take a percentage off the top from every dollar that comes from every source including theaters, in-flight entertainment, DVDs, and television licensing. This percentage can be as high as 33 percent or as low as 10 percent depending on the relative negotiating strength of each party.

Before giving the green-light, studios run the numbers to make sure that their distribution fee has a good chance of covering their outlay, even if the film itself is unprofitable for others. Once a studio provides a green-light, the studio deposits money in its account, and the production can pay all the fees and salaries necessary to make the movie.

How do studios get the money to finance this fee driven economy? To begin with, they raise a substantial part this sum by wheeling and dealing with outside parties. This includes negotiating tax credit deals around the world with financial groups needing tax relief, lease-back deals on copyright of the titles, pre-sales agreements to sell rights to foreign markers, product placement deals with corporations to insert their product or brands in their films, and hedge fund investments. This deal-making employs a large part of the entertainment law establishment who churn out the necessary paperwork. It also often provides, depending on the film, between 20 and 60 percent of the budget. For the balance of the money, studios either use their cash flow from previous films or borrow from banks through their revolving lines of credit at banks, called "revolvers," assuming, based on their financial analysis, that they will earn back this portion of the outlay from their own distribution fee.

Of course, sometimes studios miscalculate and lose money. So do independent production companies, which lack the fee rake-off. And *Sahara* famously lost money— at least for its production company and its owner, billionaire Philip Anschutz. But not for everyone who worked on it. The actors, extras, make-up artists, hair stylists, costumers, assistant directors, set designers, animal wranglers, carpenters, cameramen, grips, editors, musicians, dialogue coaches, sound engineers, caterers, drivers, and publicists all got paid. The stars, director, and writers also got their fixed compensation (though they may never see any part of their contingent compensation, or profit participation). Paramount, which distributed the movie, got its fee. Clive Cussler even got his $10 million. And of course the lawyers on both sides got their fee, as did this expert witness.

PART V
UNORIGINAL SIN

AUDIENCE CREATION

In Hollywood, originality is anything but a virtue. Paramount rejected a recent project that had attached stars, an approved script, and a bankable director by telling the producer: "It's a terrific idea, too bad it has not been made into a movie already or we could have done the remake." This response, alas, is not untypical. Studios today, as a former executive explained, tend to green-light four types of movies for wide openings: remakes (such as *King Kong*), sequels (such as *Star Wars: Episode III*), television spin-offs (such as *Mission: Impossible*), or video game extensions (such as *Lara Croft: Tomb Raider*).

If Hollywood is originality-challenged, it is not because studio executives find particular joy in mindlessly imitating bygone successes, or lack imagination. It is because they must take into account the underlying reality of today's entertainment economy. In the prior system (1928–1950), each studio was identified with a particular genre of movie: MGM (musicals and romantic comedies); Paramount (historical epics); Warner Bros. (gangster stories); 20th Century Fox (social dramas); Universal

149

(horror movies); Disney (cartoons), and just the mention of a studio star like Clark Gable or Carole Lombard on a marquee was enough to guarantee a full house. To this end, a studio could rely on a vast habitual herd of moviegoers to go to the movies in an average week. Most of these people went to see not just a new movie—the main attraction—but also a program of weekly entertainment that included newsreels, a slapstick short, a cliffhanger serial, a "B" feature, such as a Western, and needed no national advertising to prod it. That was before TV provided an alternative source of entertainment.

After TV robbed the studios of 80 percent their audience and an anti-trust suit forced them to divest themselves of their captive theaters, it was a different story. The studio names meant little, if anything at all, to audiences. Nor can the weekly movie audience, which has shrunk to less than 10 percent of the population, be relied on to show up for any particular movie. Studios therefore had to create audiences from scratch for each and every film. For the studios, "audience creation" has become just as important a creative product as the film itself.

Multiplex owners know that the six major studios can supply not only a movie, but the publicity campaign capable of driving a herd of moviegoers from their homes to the theater on an opening weekend. The studios have this capacity because, unlike independent film producers, they control when, where, and how the movie will be released, starting from the day it goes into production. With this control, the studios can shape the movie to fit the requisites of the marketing campaign, fusing both product and publicity, like Siamese twins, into a single entity. This carefully calibrated movie product can then be used to recruit multimillion-dollar merchandising tie-ins, such as with McDonald's. The studios can also insert "teasers" in the coming-attraction reels (which they control) to build audience awareness. Finally, the studios have the resources to commit up to $50 million in prerelease advertising on a single movie.

The marketing campaign has become crucial for theater owners because the names of big stars can no longer be relied on to draw a large audience unless it is incorporated into a studio-sized marketing campaign. Consider two consecutive romantic comedies with Julia Roberts, one of the highest-paid actresses; one an independent release, the other a studio release. The first, *Everyone Says I Love You*, released by Miramax, brought in $132,000 on its opening weekend. The second, *My Best Friend's Wedding*, released by Sony, brought in $21.7 million in its opening weekend. Both films had the same star actress, same genre, same romantic twist, but one film drew 150 times as many people to theaters as the other. Next, consider two consecutive movies starring Mel Gibson. The first, *What Women Want*, was released by

Paramount and brought in $33.6 million in its opening weekend, while the second, *Million Dollar Hotel*, released three months later by Lion's Gate, brought in $29,483. A thousand times as many people went to see the opening of the studio product, although both starred Gibson. Even if Roberts' *Everyone Says I Love You* and Gibson's *Million Dollar Hotel* had been vastly superior movies to their studio counterparts (and I believe they were), the results would have been the same. These films played in only a handful of theaters, while *My Best Friend's Wedding* opened on 2,134 screens and *What Women Want* opened on 3,013 screens. For the independent films to have opened "wide" as their studio counterparts did, the distributors would have had to convince the theater chains that they had the wherewithal to provide the kind of massive marketing campaign that it takes to fill 2,000 theaters with popcorn-eating audiences— a next-to-impossible undertaking.

But, unlike Hollywood's movies, the ending is not a happy one for originality. Since the publicity campaigns for these blockbusters have proven effective in the popcorn economy, studios recycle their elements into endless sequels, such as those for *Spider-Man, Pirates of the Caribbean, Shrek,* and *Mission Impossible*, which then become the studios' franchises on which they earn almost all their profits. That is their unoriginal sin and, alas, only hope of salvation in the age of streaming.

TEENS AND CAR CRASHES GO TOGETHER

After Hollywood lost its audience to television in the 1950s, it had to reinvent itself. If it could no longer count on habitual moviegoers to fill theaters routinely, it would go into the business of audience-creation. The means studios found to recruit audiences for each and every movie they released was national TV advertising. The tactic that evolved by the 1990s was bombarding a target audience with very expensive thirty-second ads. For this to work, studios had to find a demographic group that was both relatively cheap to reach and who could be induced by this blitz to leave the comfort of their home to see a movie. The audience that satisfied these conditions was teenagers.

Teens have three great advantages over adults for movie studios. First, they tend to predictably cluster around the same TV programs on cable networks, such as MTV, which make them much less costly to reach than moviegoing adults who, if they watch TV at all, tend to be scattered among the most expensive programming in prime time. Second, once in multiplexes, teens tend to consume prodigious quantities of popcorn and soda, which is a powerful attraction to the theater chains that book movies for a wide opening. Third, teens buy electronic games, sports equipment, fast food, and other licensable items, which make them an appealing audience to merchandising partners with the capability of providing the multimillion dollar "tie-in" that help publicize studio movies.

By 2009, studios had become so proficient at finding, activating, and driving the teen herd into multiplexes that over 70 percent of the audience that went to their wide release movies was under twenty-one years old. Even though the expansion of teen programming on cable and television networks allowed the studios to zero in on their target audience, they needed, as one marketing executive at Sony told me, visuals in a thirty second ad spot that would hook male teens. The movies that filled that bill were action films laden with special effects, explosions, crashes, and mayhem. Sony learned this lesson in June 2003 when it released its action movie *Hollywood Homicide*, with Harrison Ford, a $20 million star, against Universal's action movie *2 Fast 2 Furious*, a lower-budget film without any stars. *Hollywood Homicide* featured images of Harrison Ford in its thirty second ads, whereas *2 Fast 2 Furious* featured flaming car crashes. Even though *Hollywood Homicide* had done much better than *2 Fast 2 Furious* in the pre-openings awareness polls, *2 Fast 2 Furious* had a $50 million opening while *Hollywood Homicide* took in only $11.1 million. The Sony marketing executives could only conclude: Teens are more excited by car crashes than by big name stars, even one who gets a $20 million dollar paycheck. It thus became as important to cast car crashes and other violent stunts as stars in the teen-oriented remake of Hollywood.

THE MIDAS FORMULA

The studios' Midas formula may have been perfected by Steven Spielberg and George Lucas in the 1980s but the innovator was Walt Disney. He put all the elements together back in 1937, when he made *Snow White and the Seven Dwarfs*. The picture was labeled a folly by the moguls who ruled old Hollywood because it was aimed at only a small part of the American audience, children. They were wrong. *Snow White and the Seven Dwarfs*, which was re-released every seven years to a new crop of children, became the first film in history to gross $100 million. It also demonstrated to the studios, among other things, the propensity of children to see the same cartoon over and over again. The movie was also the first to have an official soundtrack, including such songs as "Some Day My Prince Will Come," that became a hit record. More important, *Snow White* had multiple licensable characters (the dwarfs, the wicked witch) who took on long lives of their own, first as toys and later as theme-park exhibits. So, here was

Hollywood's future: Its profits would come not from squeezing down the costs of producing films but from creating films with licensable properties that could generate profits in other media over long periods of time.

The advent of computer-based technology has simply provided new ways of mining this vein. The franchises that have raked in over a billion dollars from all markets (including world DVD, television, and toy licensing), *The Lord of the Rings, Harry Potter, Spider-Man, Finding Nemo, Star Wars, Shrek, The Lion King, Toy Story*, and *Pirates of the Caribbean* share most, if not all, of the nine common elements of the Midas formula:

1. They are based on children's fare stories, comic books, serials, cartoons, or, as in the case of *Pirates of the Caribbean*, a theme-park ride.
2. They feature a child or adolescent protagonist (at least in the establishing episode of the franchise).
3. They have a fairy-tale-like plot in which a weak or ineffectual youth is transformed into a powerful and purposeful hero.
4. They contain only chaste, if not strictly platonic, relationships between the sexes, with no suggestive nudity, sexual foreplay, provocative language, or even hints of consummated passion. (This ensures the movie gets the PG-13 or better rating necessary for

merchandising tie-ins and for placing ads on children's TV programming.)

5. They include characters for toy and game licensing.

6. They depict only stylized conflict—though it may be dazzling, large-scale, and noisy, in ways that are sufficiently nonrealistic and bloodless (again allowing for a rating no more restrictive than PG-13).

7. They end happily, with the hero prevailing over powerful villains and supernatural forces (and thus lend themselves to sequels).

8. They use conventional or digital animation to artificially create action sequences, supernatural forces, and elaborate settings.

9. They cast actors who are not ranking stars—at least in the sense that they do not command dollar-one gross-revenue shares.

The success of the DVD propelled the Midas-formula sequels to dazzlingly high earnings. At the height of the DVD market, a studio with a successful franchise could sell over 30 million units per sequel, harvesting for itself between $450 million and $600 million dollars. (When *Shrek 2* sold a mere 30 million copies in 2005 and had 7 million in returns—it wiped out a good portion of DreamWorks Animation's quarterly earnings.)

While this is an enormously high-stakes game, even a single successful licensing franchise can put a studio in the black—as *Spider-Man* did for Sony Pictures. Midas Formula franchises might not win Oscars, but, up until the age of streaming, they could keep the multiplexes in business.

MARKET TESTING VILLAINS

For the past decade, Hollywood has been casting financiers as the demonic villains of society. In the multiplexes, businessmen have even replaced terrorists as villains. In the Warner Bros. political thriller, *Syriana*, for example, the villain is not al-Qaeda, an enemy state, the mafia, or even a psychotic serial killer. Rather, it's the big oil companies who manipulate terrorism, wars, and social unrest to drive up oil prices. One doesn't need to look far to discover that the root-of-evil corporate villain is hardly atypical of post-Cold War Hollywood.

Consider Paramount's 2004 remake of the 1962 classic, *The Manchurian Candidate*. In the original film, directed by John Frankenheimer, the villain-behind-the-villain is the Soviet Union, whose nefarious agents, with the help of the Chinese Communists, abduct an American soldier in Korea and turn him into a sleeper assassin. In the new version, the venue is transposed from Korea in 1950 to Kuwait in 1991, and the defunct Soviet Union is replaced as the resident evil. The new villain is—you guessed it— the Manchurian Global Corporation, an American company loosely modeled on the Halliburton Corporation. As the director, Jonathan Demme, explains in his DVD commentary, he avoided making the Iraqi forces of Saddam Hussein the replacement villain, because he did not want to "negatively stereotype" Muslims. Not only were neither Saddam Hussein nor Iraq mentioned in a film about the Iraq-Kuwait war, but the Manchurian corporation's technicians rewire the brains of the abducted US soldiers with false memories of al-Qaeda-type jihadists so that they will lay the blame for terrorist acts committed by American businessmen on an innocent Muslim jihadist. So Hollywood depicts greedy corporations deluding the public about terrorism.

Why don't the movies have plausible, real world villains anymore? One reason is that a plethora of stereotype-sensitive advocacy groups, representing everyone from hyphenated ethnic minorities and physically handicapped people to Army and CIA veterans, now maintain a liaison in Hollywood to protect their image. The studios themselves often have an "outreach program" in which executives are assigned to review scripts and characters with representatives from these groups, evaluate their complaints, and attempt to avoid potential brouhahas.

Finding evil villains is not as easy as it was in the days when a director could choose among Nazis, Communists, KGB, and Mafiosos. Still, in a pinch, these old enemies will serve. For example, the 2002 apocalyptic thriller *Sum of All Fears*, based on the Tom Clancy novel in which Muslim extremists explode a nuclear bomb in Baltimore. Paramount decided, however, to change the villains to Nazi businessmen residing in South Africa to avoid offending Arab-American and Islamic groups. Yet, even if aging Nazis lack any credible "outreach program" in Hollywood, no longer can they be creditably fit into many contemporary movies since they would be in their nineties by now. "The list of non-offensive villains narrows quickly once you get past the tired clichés of Nazis," a top talent agency executive pointed out to me in an email. "You'd be surprised at how short the list is."

Since international markets now provide Hollywood with 70 percent of its revenue for action movies, studios find it increasingly risky to employ villains from potentially valuable markets such as China. Consider, for example, the MGM remake of John Mileus 1984 classic *Red Dawn* in which Chinese bad guys invade America. In the new version, which MGM plans to release in 2012, the movie has been digitally altered and re-edited to make the primary villains North Koreans. Since North Korea is one of the few countries in the world in which Hollywood does not distribute its movies, it remains on the short list of evil stereotypes.

For sci-fi and horror movies, there are always invaders from alien universes and zombies from another dimension, but even here it doesn't hurt if they are in the greed business. In the 2009 movie *Avatar*, a greedy mining corporation is behind the use of avatars to destroy the environment, culture, and natives on the planet Pandora. This proved a lucrative decision since the movie earned a large share of its revenue in foreign countries concerned about corporate exploitation of their resources and environment. But for reality-based politico-thrillers the safest remaining characters are lily-white, impeccably dressed American corporate executives. They are especially useful as evildoers in foreign-based thrillers since their demonization does not run the risk of gratuitously offending officials in countries either hosting the filming or supplying tax or production subsidies. *Mission Impossible 2* thus replaced the Russian and Chinese heavies that populated the TV series with a Wall Street-type financier who controlled a pharmaceutical company that aimed to make a fortune by unleashing a horrific virus on the world. How? It owned the antidote. Here, as in other movies in this genre, businessmen's killings are not just figurative. Unlike other stereotype-challenged groups, CEOs and financiers, lacking a connection with the studios' outreach programs, have become an essential part of Hollywood's casting. They are the new all-purpose money demons.

WHY SERIOUS FARE WENT SMALL SCREEN

Once upon a time, the television set was commonly called the "boob tube," and elites looked down on it as a purveyor of mind-numbing entertainment. Movie theaters, on the other hand, were considered a venue for, if not art, more sophisticated dramas and comedies. Not anymore. The multiplexes are now primarily a venue for dumbed down comic-book inspired action and fantasy movies, whereas television, especially the pay and cable channels, is increasingly becoming a venue for character driven adult programs, such as *The Wire, Mad Men,* and *Boardwalk Empire.* This role reversal, rather than a momentary fluke, proceeds directly from the new economic realities of the entertainment business.

When HBO was initially signing up monthly subscribers in the 1970s, it provided the only way home viewers could see movies uninterrupted by commercials, and it (and its Cinemax unit) eventually signed up 40 million subscribers through local cable systems. HBO gets a fixed fee—about $4.50 per month—for each subscriber, no matter how little or often they watch HBO. To continue to harvest this immense bounty, HBO has to perform a single feat: stop subscribers from ending their subscription. But since nowadays its subscribers can get movies cheaper and faster from other sources, such as Netflix, retail stores, and the Internet, HBO needs a more exclusive inducement to keep them. And so, beginning in the 1990s, it began putting more and more resources into creating its own original programming that would appeal to the head of the house. Not restricted by the need to maximize the audience (it has no advertising), ratings boards (it has no censorship), or non-English speaking markets, it was able to create edgy character-driven series such as *Sex and the City*, which not only succeeded in retaining their subscribers but achieved surprising acclaim in the media. Other pay-channels followed suit. So did other networks so as not lose market share. The result is the elevation of television, or at least some tiers of it, to a medium of entertainment for the elite.

Meanwhile, Hollywood, conforming to its new economic landscape, has had a gradual downgrade. Unlike in the era of the studio system in which studios opened their movies in select first-run theaters, the big six Hollywood studios nowadays open their major movies nationally on 3,500 or more screens owned by a handful of multiplex chains. The deal-breaking issue for the strategists is not the intrinsic merits of the film but whether it contains the necessary elements to attract a target audience of tweens and teens who also are the group most likely to consume popcorn, candy, and soda. With this targeted audience in its sights, the marketing executives tend to only approve movies that contain elements that, when encapsulated in ads, will activate these young people to go to the movies, such as visually-stunning action. Even so, since anything original is chancy, marketing executives lean towards formulas that have been successfully used before; hence, the profusion of action movie sequels.

In addition, studios need to consider another part of the new economic landscape: the growing importance of non-English speaking markets. Nowadays major Hollywood releases earn most of their revenue abroad, and large scale action films, such as *Avatar*, *Spider-Man 3*, and *Mission Impossible 3* earn more than 70 percent of their revenue in overseas markets. Since many of these foreign territories depend on dubbing, especially in Asia and Latin America, studios have found that the formula for successful bookings is, as a top Fox executive put it, "Short on dialogue, long on action." Happily for the studios, this formula fits with the requisites for marketing to its target audience in America. Add to this equation the multiplexes' appetite for supersized 3D movies (which lets them jack up ticket prices), and it is hardly surprising that Hollywood is moving more and more towards comic-book sequels and other action-bumped fantasy fare. Meanwhile television, which must to adopt to a new Internet world in which its audience can cherry-pick what it wants to see, anytime and anywhere, via ubiquitous DVRs, tablets, and computers, is now providing the sophisticated niche entertainment that movies once provided.

PART VI
INDIE FILM

THE OSCAR DECEPTION

Each year a global audience, second in size only to the Super Bowl, watches television's most lucrative infomercial: the Annual Academy Awards. For some three and a half hours, interspersed with clips from currently-available movies, Hollywood's most publicized stars will ecstatically award the winners 13-inch-high gold-dipped statuettes known the world over as the Oscars.

The initial purpose of this gala event, which the studios created along with the Academy of Motion Picture Arts and Sciences in 1927, was, in the words of its main architect Louis B. Mayer, "to establish the industry in the public's mind as a respectable institution." But it was also designed to market and create "stars." Mayer was cofounder of Metro-Goldwyn-Mayer, one of Hollywood's most successful studios during its Golden Age (1930s–1950s) and is known as the father of Hollywood's "star system" of marketing.

The stars come out for Oscar night, but to further enhance its global audience in 2010, the Academy doubled the number of Best Picture nominees. Even with this expansion, attention remained focused on two polar opposite films: Kathryn Bigelow's *The Hurt Locker*, and James Cameron's *Avatar*, both of which garnered eight other Oscar nominations.

The Hurt Locker is a reality-based film about a squad of courageous American soldiers who defuse bombs under horrendous conditions in Iraq. By Hollywood standards, it is a very small movie, costing only $15 million to produce and another $15 million to publicize and distribute. And although critically acclaimed, it sold only $50 million in tickets worldwide. With theaters keeping roughly half of these box-office sales and the distributor deducting its expenses off the top, it remains in the red. Nevertheless, for many among the Academy's nearly 6,000 voting members, it represents the kind of intelligent realism that Hollywood is capable of making for an adult audience.

Avatar, on the other hand, is a fantasy-based movie about alien life forms who need to be rescued from neocolonialist corporate exploitation on a planet called Pandora. The film, enhanced by brilliant visual effects, may be the most expensive ever made. According to a top executive at Fox, it cost over $225 million to produce and another $150 million to publicize and distribute—a number that has been hyped to as much as a half-billion dollars.

Whatever the cost, *Avatar* has been an immense success, selling a record-breaking $750 million of tickets in the US, where it is shown in 3D as well as the traditional 2D format, and more than twice that amount overseas, where it's shown mainly in 2D.

For Rupert Murdoch's 20th Century Fox, which gets its distribution fee off the top (as well Dune Entertainment and Ingenious Partners, the private equity funds that provided 60% of the financing, and James Cameron's production company, Lightstorm Entertainment) it is a gold mine.

The film's success at the box office has also excited hopes that its 3D visual effects will restore the Golden Age of movie attendance, a time before television when two-thirds of Americans went to the movies in an average week.

The overall box-office numbers, however, provide little grounds for such optimism. *Avatar* no doubt has enriched many theaters charging a premium for the 3D experience, but it did so largely at the expense of theaters showing other movies. In the eight weeks that *Avatar* dominated US box-office receipts, total movie attendance increased by about 6 percent.

But even if the audience resurgence is no more than a pipe dream, *Avatar* represents for many in the Academy the idea that Hollywood's ultimate salvation lies not in superior story-telling and acting but in eye-popping visual effects, stunning animation and state-of-the-art 3D projection that immerse the audience in the illusion.

Regardless of box office receipts, Hollywood's major studios have a sure-fire engine for making money from viewers who don't regularly go to the movies. It's what the studio calls its "library," which contains the rights to all the movies and television series that it has ever produced or acquired. By relentlessly licensing and selling the rights to these titles, studios harvest money from home audiences decades after a film plays in theaters.

Consider, for example, the Time Warner library. It has more than 45,000 hours of feature movies, cartoons and TV episodes, dubbed or subtitled in more than 40 languages, that it licenses to pay-tv, cable TV, satellite telecasters and television stations in more than 175 countries. These titles are often bundled in take-it-or-leave-it packages (a practice that is prohibited by US anti-trust laws in distributing movies to theaters), which helps optimize profits. In 2009, just the television distribution part of this operation brought in more than $2 billion, according to one source at Warner Brothers. A revenue stream this lucrative, even after paying residuals to guilds, labor and other participants, would be enough to pay for most, if not all, the costs of Warner Brothers' new movies.

Libraries, of course, also pull in huge revenues from the global sale and rental of DVDs. (Technically, newly released titles are not included in the library for two years.) Even though DVD sales of movie titles and TV series are now waning, on the horizon is another promising revenue stream: digital rights for Internet delivery. While at present these rights provide little more than pocket change for studios, future revenues are due to explode with the proliferation of smart phones, netbooks, tablets, game consoles and other such gadgets. In any case, as one Viacom executive recently told me, "No studio could stay solvent for long without a library."

If the studios' libraries, the reality-based money machines that boost the bottom line, do not receive accolades or even a mention at Sunday's Academy Awards, it isn't that their value is unappreciated. It's because Hollywood's real genius is understanding that its audience prefers illusion to reality. The stars shine brightest on Oscar night. And that's show business.

CAN INDIE MOVIES SURVIVE?

If you are a producer of indie movies, the great sucking sound you may be hearing is *Avatar* draining money from your future projects. While this brilliant *Pocahontas* meets-*Jurassic Park* mashup may be a bonanza for Rupert Murdoch's 20th Century Fox studio, which gets a distribution fee on every dollar it brings in from theaters, video stores, and TV, and its producer-director James Cameron, who gets a cut of the gross after it reached its Hollywood defined $500 million cash break-even point, it will further convince the heads of the major studios that their salvation lies in putting their money in "high value" movies laden with mesmerizing visual effects that can be simultaneously opened on more than 5,000 screens around the world and lend themselves to sequels, merchandise tie-ins, toy licensing, and theme park rides.

To be sure, even before the phenomenal success of *Avatar*, the Big Six studios were shying away from smaller movies despite their potential profits. Consider, for example, the sad story told to me by one of the most successful indie producers in New York. In 2009, he brought a major studio a $20 million project packaged with a hot director and two stars. After running the numbers, the studio estimated that its potential box-office in America at $100 million, which would yield it, just from its 30 percent distribution fee and a locked-in output deal with HBO, a 100 percent profit on its investment. But it turned down the project. One of the studio's top executives told the producer, "We don't do films that do not have a projected box-office of at least $150 million."

The reason for this rule is that a studio has only a limited number of slots for its releases at multiplexes and it has to fill them with projects, whether profitable or not, that generate maximum revenue, since the slice it takes off the top in the form of distribution fee pays the studio's overhead (which includes the executive's six-figure paycheck). This means worldwide grosses—almost

75 percent of *Avatar* ticket sales is from foreign audience—and indie films even if they are profitable, cannot be counted on to do that job.

Unlike a studio producer, an indie producer rarely, if ever, has a U.S. distribution deal in advance of shooting. To raise the money to shoot a film, he or she must either find an outside investor, an equity partner, or get a bank loan. What made loans possible, at least up until recently, were the availability of pre-sales agreements. These odd devices, which had been the backbone of indie financing since Dino de Laurentiis invented them in the 1970s, worked as follows: an indie produced would sell the distribution rights in foreign territories and then use the contracts as collateral to borrow from banks. Foreign buyers were willing to sign pre-sales deals because they assumed the film would get U.S. distribution since up until 2008 there was no shortage of smaller distributors specializing in indie films, including Miramax, Fox Searchlight, Fox Atomic Films, Paramount Vantage,
Warner Independent Pictures, Picturehouse, New Line, Fine Line Features, Focus Features, Sony Pictures Classics, Lionsgate, the Weinstein Company, and Summit Entertainment.

Since the cash flows from indie films tends to be erratic, these smaller distributors had come to rely on advance output deals with three pay-tv channels—HBO, Showtime, and Starz—to pay their overhead. In return, the pay channels got the exclusive rights to show their new movies. In 2008, for example, the $80 million that New Line Cinema received from HBO paid its annual overhead and development costs. Bob Weinstein, the cochairman of the Weinstein Company, not only described output deals as "the bedrock of the business," but said in 2008 "not one company in this business could survive and succeed without one."

His words soon proved prophetic. When the pay channels found they needed fewer movie titles to retain subscribers and began cutting back on their output deals in 2008, the "bedrock" crumbled within a matter of months. By 2010, most of these indie distributors and mini-majors were effectively out of business including New Line Cinema, Fine Line Features, Picturehouse, Warner Independent, Fox Atomic, and Paramount Vantage. Miramax, the linchpin of indie distribution for nearly two decades, closed down its main office in New York in 2008, and in 2010 its owner, Walt Disney, sold the company and its library to Filmyard Holdings for more than $660 million. Almost all remaining players have drastically changed their acquisition strategy. Sony Pictures Classics does not buy any film that costs over $2 million, Focus Features is putting its resources mainly in co-production deals in Asia, and Lionsgate is investing in horror sequels like *Saw VII*. With the prospect of American distribution rapidly fading, indie producers are now finding pre-sale financing almost impossible. "It's a dead business model," a former Miramax executive said.

If so how can Indie producers continue to make movies?   The answer turned out to be streamers. Anthony Bregman, who had produced over thirty independent films, including *Ice storm, Thumbsucker* and *The Eternal Sunshine of the Spotless Mind,* explained to me in 2017 that he was now only making films for Netflix and other streamers because making movies for theaters "no longer made financial sense" while streamers could not only pay for the production of their films but guarantee that they reached an audience. Hollywood distributors could do neither.

HOW TO FINANCE AN INDIE FILM

The first reality an indie producer must come to grips with is that it is almost impossible to get meaningful US distribution for a movie before it is made, even if the producer has a great script, cast, and director. This means that for all practical purposes the value of the US market for financing a movie is virtually zero.

As a result, a producer has to depend almost entirely on the foreign markets for financing. To be sure, foreign distributors, no longer confident that indie films would have the publicity and hype that goes with an American release, have greatly reduced the amount they are willing to commit, and three of the top seven markets, Japan, Spain, and Italy, have sharply cut back on their pre-sales deals, but even so, it is possible to raise the additional funds through government subsidies and tax shelters (which can provide 30 percent of the budget). Assume that the producer has lined up all the ingredients necessary for international sales, including script, director, and stars, and now needs $10 million to make the movie. Here is what must be done.

STEP I: FOREIGN PRE-SALES

The producer first must retain a foreign sales agent to sell the foreign territories. This agent, who gets between

10 and 20 percent of these sales, makes an assessment of what these markets are worth, then negotiates contracts in which each foreign distributor agrees to pay the producer an agreed upon sum once the movie is actually delivered.

In return, he gets all theatrical, DVD, electronic, and television rights to the territory until receipts exceed this sum. The best a producer can hope for these days from the foreign markets is 80 percent of budget, so, if all goes well, the producer of this $10 million film gets $8 million in contracts for foreign sales.

STEP II: SUBSIDIES

The producer arranges to shoot the film in a state or country that provides "soft money" in the form of subsidies and tax credits for about 30 percent of budget, which, in this case, will yield another $3 million. To get this money, however, he or she has to complete the movie. Even though on paper, the producer now has $11 million to make a $10 million movie, he or she needs to convert it to cash. This requires finding a bank willing to accept these pieces of paper as collateral. But no bank will do so without another piece of paper, called a completion bond. The completion bond guarantees that the movie, come hell or high water, will be completed and delivered with all the elements, such as stars, specified in the contracts.

STEP III: COMPLETION BOND

The producer buys a completion bond from an issuer such as Film Finance. The company, to reduce its risk, insists on certain conditions. Typically, it requires a producer put aside 10 percent of the budget for unexpected contingencies as well the money necessary for so-called "deliverables," such as the dupe negatives for foreign distributors. In the case of this $10 million film, the completion bond company takes a 2.6 percent fee, or $260,000, and requires $1 million for the "contingencies" and $200,000 for the "deliverables" be held in an escrow account, once the bank delivers the loan.

STEP IV: BANK FINANCING

Banks, even with a completion bond, will lend no more than 80 percent of the face value of the collateral. In this case, the producer borrows 80 percent on the $11 million in contracts and soft money, or $8.8 million. But from that sum, the bank deducted its own fee, which is 3 percent, or $264,000. In addition, it also requires that the producer set aside in an escrow account the interest on the loan for 18 months. At a blended rate of five percent, this amounts to $660,000. So what the producer actually gets is only $7,876.000.

Now, once the loan is delivered, the producer must pay the foreign sales agent. Assume the agent gets a 15 percent fee of the $8 million in pre-sales, or $1,200,000.

The producer now has only $6,676,00. Then, after paying completion bond company, and putting the requisite money aside for contingencies and deliverables, he or she has $5,216,000 left from the loan, barely half the money needed to shoot the $10 million movie.

STEP V: FINANCING THE GAP

Filling a nearly $5 million gap is no easy matter. If the producer reduces the budget by cutting out any of the stars or other specified production values, he will violate the terms of the pre-sales and subsidy contracts. So unless he wants to re-negotiate with everyone, he has to stick to the budget. Nor can he borrow more money against the bankable collateral since he has mortgaged his production to the hilt.

This leaves the producer only one way to fill the gap: finding an equity investor to buy part of a movie that has not yet made. To make such a "gap" investment feasible, the producer can offer the investor repayment from the 20 percent tier of the foreign contracts and subsidy contracts not covered by the bank loan. In this case, that 20 percent tier will yield $2,200,000 after the film is delivered in all the foreign markets. But that still leaves an unsecured risk of some $3 million. If the producer manages to bring the movie in on budget, the $1 million fund held for contingencies can also be used to further repay the equity investor. But the investor still has $2 million at risk. To get back this money, and make a profit, he must gamble that the unsold American rights will be sold after the movie is completed. Since of the thousands of movies submitted to film festivals each year, only a few dozen find meaningful distribution, this is no small risk. But resourceful producers can find investors willing to take it.

PART VII

DANCING ON THE EDGE OF THE DIGITAL ABYSS

THE QUEST FOR THE DIGITALIZED
COUCH POTATO

At the dawn of the age of streaming, the numbers—
or at least the secret studio revenue numbers in the
May 2008 *All Media Revenue Report*—foretold the
story. As late as 1980, movie theaters provided the
studios with 55 percent of their total revenues; in
2007, movie theaters provided only 20 percent of
their total revenue (over half of which came from
overseas). The other 80 percent now came from the
ubiquitous couch potato who was viewing his
movies at home via DVDs, Blu-rays, pay-per-view,
a digital recorder, cable channels, or even network
television. A studio's task in this environment, as
Sony Chairman Howard Stringer explained to me,
"is to optimally leverage our product across all
these [new] platforms." The way studios achieve
this "optimal leverage" was to give each of these
platforms a discrete time frame, or window in
which it could exploit the home audience.

A brief history is in order. Since the 1980s, the
studios have managed their revenue by employing a
system of "windows" to release their products to
different markets.

First, movies play in theaters, then, six months
later, the video window opens, followed by the

opening of the pay-tv and then free television window.

Then at the turn of the millennium the prospect of mass sales of DVDs in retail stores began opening cracks in the entire system. Warner Bros. led the way. To win critical shelf space in Wal-Marts, they needed to release their summer blockbusters such as *Harry Potter* and *Batman* on DVD during the hottest sales periods, Thanksgiving to Christmas, instead of waiting for an artificial window to open up later. So they shortened their window. Other studios followed suit with a vengeance, shrinking the window to four, or in some cases even three, months. Then thanks to the Internet, studios began to announce an upcoming DVD while the movie was still playing in theaters. As a top studio executive explained to me, "It was a voluntary decision made for purely financial reasons by the major players . . . to satisfy quarterly profit goals, nothing more, nothing less." To avoid losing audiences, multiplex chains, which need to maximize their popcorn sales to stay in business, cut the run of such movies. The consequence was a spiral that fed on itself: the shorter the run, the less money from the box office. This decrease, in turn, further increased pressure from the young Turks in the studios' home-entertainment divisions to further collapse the window. The main resistance to this change came from the old-guard studio executives who fear that undercutting the movie-theater business will—even if it improves DVD sales—unravel the very foundations of Hollywood. They argued that the theatrical platform, to which most of the PR hoopla, magazine covers, TV talk shows, and the rest of the celebrity-worshiping culture is geared, is crucial to generate worldwide DVD sales. The $64 billion question for the studios became: Does any barrier, no less a fragile window, make sense in the quest for the couch potato in an increasingly digital age?

Amidst this battle to devise a strategy for the DVD window, the entire window faced an emerging existential threat in the form of digital downloading. Even though it took more time than most consumers were willing to spend, a movie could be downloaded from the global Internet. The only barrier to widespread use was the time it took to transfer a massive video file from one computer to another. When this bottleneck to delivery was reduced, the artificial boundaries between pay-tv, network television and cable television would be rendered   irrelevant.

THE SAMURAI EMBRACE

The momentous shift from theaters to homes proceeded from a series of decisions made not in Hollywood or New York, but in Tokyo and Osaka. The hand of Tokyo, though not always be visible in the dazzling glitter of Hollywood, pushed the film industry further into the world of the couch potato. It is not that the Japanese set out to change the way the world sees movies, it is that Hollywood failed to see its own digital destiny lay in home entertainment. This reinvention of the film business began in the 1970s with the engineering by Sony and Matsushita of an affordable videocassette recorder. Through a process of ingenious compromises, Sony made its Betamax small enough to fit on top of a TV set and foolproof enough to be operated by a child. The Hollywood studios led by Universal fought for seven years in the courts to prevent it from reaching the market.

If they had prevailed over Sony, the video rental market may never have developed, but, fortunately for the studios, they lost their case in the Supreme Court in 1984. (It was a bittersweet victory for Sony who, in the interim, lost the format war to the even more user-friendly VHS format developed by Matsushita.)

The VCR soon became a ubiquitous household appliance, video stores became a part of the urban landscape and the newfound flow of money from video rentals proved to be financial salvation for the very studios that had so bitterly fought the new technology. As a consequence, in deciding what films to make, studios approved projects that had greater potential for huge video rentals. These proved to be special-effects laden disaster and fantasy films that appealed to children and teenagers. Films that did not fit the requisites of video buyers were given a lower priority and, as it turned out, these included dramas, comedies and political exposés intended for an older, more diverse, and less predictable audience.

Next, in the mid-1990s, Toshiba and Sony changed the Hollywood equation even more radically by substituting a digital platform, the "DVD" for the videocassette. As with the VCR, this digital future was resisted by most of the Hollywood studios who were concerned that it might kill the video business that had become their golden goose. But now Sony, which owned the Columbia Tristar studio, and Toshiba, which was a part owner (and strategic partner) of the Warner Bros. studio, had marshaled enough power in Hollywood to ensure that enough titles would be available for the DVD launch. The combined libraries of these two studios included over 24,000 titles. So, in August 1995, in a conference in Hawaii, Sony and Toshiba (and all the other Japanese manufacturers) agreed on a single format.

Even though most of the other major studios did not participate, the DVD roll-out succeeded in transforming films into a retail product. DVDs could be played not only on DVD players, but on personal computers, game consoles, iPods, and other digital devices. By 2000, Walmart had become Hollywood's single biggest customer, selling about a third of all DVDs, occasioning top studio executives to journey to Bentonville, Arkansas, to find out what ratings, stars, genres, and other attributes would help them win strategic placement in Wal-Mart stores.

Throughout the 1990s studios had been cutting back on the number of titles they released since the popcorn culture at the multiplexes did not require much diversity. But now retailers such as Wal-Mart, Target, and Borders allocated valuable shelf space according to the numbers of titles a studio could deliver. As shelf space became the new name of the game, studios sought to increase their leverage, or throw weight, by buying up independent distributors (and later "mini-majors") to get more titles. As a result, six companies—Time Warner, Sony, Fox, Viacom, Disney, and Universal—came to dominate not only all the major releases but the entire universe of so-called indie releases. The DVD, with its random access and easy navigation, also opened up for these companies a rich new market: boxed sets of TV series. Not only could they tap their huge TV libraries, but they could invest in original series, such as *The Sopranos, Mad Men, Big Love, The Wire, Rome, Dexter, Sex and the City*, and *24*, which often proved more profitable than films that opened in theaters.

For the growing home audience, the DVD also made films a more interactive experience. Couch potatoes could now change the language of a film, its aspect ratio, rating, or ending; watch additional scenes (which in some cases are shot for the DVD), or listen to commentaries by directors, writers, and actors, or play a game, music video, or gag reel. With these bonus features driving a large part of DVD sales—one-third of polled DVD buyers said that they first played the bonus feature—Hollywood's films became part of a package.

The next move by the Japanese electronics giants came in 2005: the high-definition disc. Pioneered by Japanese television in the late 1970s, high definition makes the home the equivalent of a theater by furnishing film-like images on a large screen. There were two versions, Toshiba's HD-DVD and Sony's Blu-ray.

Since both render a similar quality image, the battle between Sony and Toshiba turned on who could enroll Hollywood studios in support of their format. And, as the Japanese manufacturers knew from their past format wars, this would require bribes in the form of "replication deals." Sony had an advantage in that it owned one of the major studios, Sony Pictures. It then bought control of MGM—almost exclusively for the purpose of locking its library into the Blu-ray formula. And it made secret deals with Disney and Fox, giving it four studios with about half of Hollywood's desirable titles. Toshiba fought back by spending over a quarter of billion dollars in cash replication deals, getting for its money Paramount, Universal, and Dreamworks to commit to exclusively put their titles on Toshiba's HD-DVD format. The format war was then decided by Warner Bros., which sold almost 40 percent of all DVDs. Its CEO, Jeff Bewkes, decided its interest lay in establishing a single format, and opted for Blu-ray.

Meanwhile, Sony launched PlayStation 3, which despite its juvenile sounding name, is a state-of-the-art computer that can connect wirelessly to TV sets, computers, printers, and the Internet, and simultaneously run up to nine different kinds of consumer electronics, play and record high-definition films, download movies from the Internet and (with a card) cable television, and, as far as games go, render characters in frighteningly realistic ways. The result was further convergence of Hollywood's dream factory with the digital domain of the Internet.

THE RISE OF THE TUBE MOGULS

As the drive to take win the home audience accelerated, Hollywood turned over its studios to television executives. Robert Iger, former head of ABC television, replaced the movie mogul Michael Eisner at Disney. Brad Grey, the former head of a television production company, Brillstein Grey Entertainment, became the studio head at Paramount. Howard Stringer, a former president of CBS Television, became the first non-Japanese chairman of Sony. Peter Chernin, a former president of Fox broadcasting, became chairman of the Fox Entertainment Group, which includes the Twentieth-Century Fox studio. Robert C. Wright, the former head of NBC television, became head of NBC Universal, which owns the Universal studio. And Jeff Bewkes, the head of HBO, became CEO and chairman of Time Warner. That all of Hollywood's new moguls have come from the realm of television reflects a singular if dismal reality: in 2009, only about 2 percent of Americans went to the movies on a given day, whereas more than 90 percent of them watched something on television at home.

Moreover, the shift to home entertainment is gathering momentum as couch potatoes find more convenient ways to obtain movies in a high-definition format. Netflix had come into picture, and in its first year 2009, had streamed millions of movies and TV episodes into homes. Amazon was also moving into streaming. DVDS distribution was also offering more convenient and cheaper rentals through vending machines. Redbox, for example, which was offering movies on DVDs at 99 cents per night, accounted for almost one-third of DVD rentals in 2009. Since the average ticket at the multiplex costs over $7, this new 99-cent rental price could induce more and more people to skip the theater. The movie theater audience was rapidly becoming reduced to teens who want to get out of their homes on weekends, and while sizable, that niche audience was no longer the major profit center for the Hollywood studios. Theatrical releases, despite the blinding allure they held for the media, now served essentially as launching platforms for videos, DVDs, network TV, pay-tv, games, and a host of other home entertainment products.

This transformation was not necessarily bad news for Hollywood's big six studios. Ever since the 1970s, they have produced the largest share of television's most successful series, including such hits as the various *CSI* shows. Their immense libraries syndicate or license to cable networks and local stations most of their movies and television shows, and they earn a royalty from each movie sent out at Netflix, as well as licensing fees on moves rented at Blockbuster and other video store chains. Even Redbox pays the studio the same wholesale price as other video stores (about 65 percent of the retail price). Consequently, studios took to promoting executives who are more experienced with the home audience than with the vanishing movie-theater audience.

TAKING OVER HOLLYWOOD, ITALIAN STYLE

At our initial meeting at the fashionable L'Circe restaurant in New York in 1990, Giancarlo Parretti had philosophized "life is like a movie. You can look at the parts you like." The version that he preferred is a heroic saga that traces his meteoric rise from working as waiter, against all odds, to owning Hollywood studios. Over a lavish lobster dinner, he described his game plan for controlling the international film business.

A few weeks earlier, Parretti had stunned Wall Street by bidding $1.2 billion in cash for MGM/UA-- a movie company which both Rupert Murdoch and Ted Turner had looked at only months before but decided not to make an offer. Even more surprising, in the documents he filed with the SEC, he specified no source for where the money was coming from-- other than an "oral, non-binding agreement" for $200 million with an unnamed company-- and he did not even have an investment banker. "I do not need Wall Street's money", he told one New York investment banker attempting to offer his services to him, "I can get one billion, two billion, whatever I need from European banks".

His own history was also stunning. As late as 1982, he was an employee of a fish processing factory in Hong Kong. Now, a would-be hero From zero, he claimed an empire that included movie studios, theaters, film laboratories, distributors, and production companies. In 1988, he bought the oldest film company in France, Pathe S.A., as well as the Hollywood studio, Cannon Films, which was best known for Ninja and vengeance fantasies (and which he re-named Pathe Communications). From that point on, at a breath-taking pace, he made announced a new multi-million dollar deal almost every month. In December 1988, it was a $160 million film production contract for Menachin Golan, the Israeli entrepreneur, who with his Israeli cousin, Yorus Globus, built Cannon into a trans-oceanic film maker. In January 1989, he announced a $80 million plan to bail out the famed Italian producer Dino Delaurentiis by buying his bankrupt movie studio so he could merge it into his own. In February, he made a $138 million offer for the television production company New World Films. In March, he made a $39 million offer for the arty

Kings Road Films. In April, he first floated the idea of taking over MGM for a cool billion. In May, he had bid $220 for Television Monte Carlo, which owned an Italian TV network.

As it turned out, none of these announced deals had been actually consummated. He aborted the Golem production deal a few months after it was announced. The financier Ronald Perelman outbid him for New World. The Kings Road deal fell apart. The Dino de Laurentius rescue mission failed. MGM accepted a bid from an Australian suitor, Quinex (which then failed to make the down payment and went bankrupt.) The Television Monte Carlo deal also never got off the ground. And, adding insult to injury, the French government blocked his acquisition of Pathe SA because he had not accurately represented the principals behind the deal. But now in 1990, he found another $1.2 billion to buy MGM. Where did the money come from?

In Hollywood, Parretti lived in Great Gatsby style. He bought a $8 mansion in Beverly Hills, where he proudly took me to his walk-in steel vault to see paintings he identifies as Picassos, Miros and Goyas. He lived there with Maria Ceccone, who he has been married to for over 20 years, two daughters and son and Fabio Serena, his 35 year old lawyer. He also leased a $200,000 Rolls Royce for driving around town, and owned a great Italian restaurant, Maderos, on the ground floor of the CMA building with a private satellite hook-up to get Italian soccer games. He also owned a disco in Hollywood called Tramps.

Like the hero of Gogol's "Dead Souls", who spawns rumor after rumor about himself as he moves through the Russian provinces trying to buy up rights to deceased serfs to further a financial scheme, Parretti, trying to buy up near-dead film companies, had stirred the collective imagination of Hollywood. "The word is the Mafia is behind him," a top agent suggested to me; "Parretti is a creature of Credit Lyonnaise," a studio executive theorized to me, sent to America to salvage the bank's bad loans to Cannon, De Laurentiis, New World and other shaky Hollywood producers. "Parretti is laundering money for the drug cartel," a Hollywood investment banker told me, pointing out that movie theaters are cash businesses, and what Parretti has bought in Cannon and Pathe is 800 movie theaters. "He is fronting for Silvio Berlusconi," the Milanese media king, an Italian director confided in me, adding, "It's Qaddafi's oil money" The proliferation of Parretti rumors did not sit well with Alan Ladd, Jr., who since January 1989 has been Pathe's co-chairman. Like his father in the movie "Shane," he wasted no words. "It's all I hear. And its complete garbage", he said, leaning forward on the couch of his plush new office at Pathe Communications on San Vincenzo Drive. He had met Parretti at the home of Dino De Laurentius in late 1988, and immediately accepted his offer to head Pathe. Next to him sat his longtime associate at the Ladd Company, Jay Canter-- Marlon Brando's first agent-

- who is vice president of Pathe. Both men were now in the odd position of having to defend a stranger who they had met only a few months earlier. Shaking his head in disbelief, Ladd cited the recent allegation in newspapers that Parretti was involved with the Qaddafi. He explained "The reporter mixed up two countries-- Liberia, where Parretti had a shipping businesses and Libya". Parretti had nothing to do with Libya or Qaddafi, Ladd insisted. He found the Mafia money whispers equally absurd. Why would the Mob put money in someone as "high-profile" as Parretti, he asked. "Don't you think I investigated before I took this job? He explained that in the Spring of 1989 he went to Europe with him in his gulfstream, which, he recalled, was equipped with a kitchen where Parretti cooked spaghetti for everyone. During the trip, Parretti handed Ladd a telephone-size book listing the hotels in the Melia chain, which he claimed he owned. "There were hundreds of hotels, and each of them represented real money", Ladd recounts. He in fact sat in at a At a press conference in Cannes where Parretti suggested that these hotels earned $300 million a year. There is "no mystery" where Parretti money comes from, Ladd concluded.

As it turned out, however, Parretti had never owned the Melia hotel chain. Nor did he own it when he handed Ladd the impressive Melia book. What had happened was that he, together with others, had bought the Melia Group in 1987 but the hotels themselves, which were the main asset, were almost immediately resold to the Sol Hotel chain in a complicated transaction that left Parretti and his associate owning only the name "Melia" and a few Spanish travel agencies and laundries that lost money and were deeply in debt. According to the 1988 annual report of his entire holding company, which included the "Melia Group", its net worth was not anything like the $1.5 billion figure he reported to *Variety*, but $3.6 million (and even this meager total is based on questionable evaluations of illiquid investment.) Instead of his businesses making an annual profit of "$300 million," as he claimed at the press conference-- or a cumulative profit of a billion dollars as he claimed in an interview in the Italian newspaper, *La Republica*-- they had, according to this annual report, actually lost money in both 1986 and 1987. It, moreover, had only $9000 in its bank accounts and in short-term funds at the end of 1987 (the last time it filed an annual report). But if the Melia hotels did not supply Parretti with the $60 million he used in his Hollywood buying spree, where did he get it?

Who was Parretti? According to his birth certificate, Giancarlo Parretti was born on October 26, 1940 in the town of Orvieto, Umbria, about 100 miles north of Rome. His father, whom he introduced to Ladd, had been a humble wine merchant (and still lived modestly in an apartment in Orvieto). At the age of 17, without the benefit of any higher education, Parretti went to work as a waiter. During the sixties, he says, he learned English working as a ship's steward on the Queen Elizabeth and as a waiter at the Savoy Hotel in

London (though neither the Cunard Lines nor the Savoy Hotel could find any record of his employment). Then Parretti moved to Sicily where he got a job waiting in a plush hotel in Syracusa owned by Palermo's political boss, Senator Graziano Verzotto. By 1973, he had worked his way up to being manager of the hotel and the aide de camp to Senator Verzotto. Senator Verzotto, who owned Syracusa's football team and supervised Sicily's state owned mineral company, then got into serious trouble. He was indicted for embezzling $3 million dollars from the mineral company in Sicily and, to make matters worse, was nearly gunned down by a team of presumably Mafia hit men. In 1975, he fled to Lebanon, leaving Parretti in charge of his hotels and the soccer team.

After Verzotto disappeared, Parretti went into the business of publishing weekly news letters, called "Diario". Beginning first in Sicily, Parretti then went in partners with Ceasare de Michealis, a key financier for the Parti Socialist Italia, or PSI, which in coalition with the larger Christian Democrat Party, had run Italy since World war II. Even though most of these "Diarios" had a circulation of under a thousand readers, they carried advertising from businessmen-- including those who wanted to curry favor with the PSI, which was a far more entrepreneurial organization than its name might imply. It had responsibility, within the political coalition that ran Italy, for overseeing a number of Italian state-owned enterprises including ENI-- the Italian equivalent Exxon combined with Dupont, which was the country's single largest generator of wealth and foreign exchange.

Parretti here had a crucially important connection: his partner's brother, Gianni de Michealis, now Italy's Foreign Minister, who then, as the PSI's Minister for State Participations, was in charge of ENI. De Michealis, a long-haired, jowly-faced intellectual, whose extra-curriculum interest is international discotheques (a subject on which he wrote a book), was in the late 1970s, because of his responsibility for ENI, one of the most powerful men in the PSI. By hitching his wagon to this rising star, Parretti moved into the inner sanctum of the party. He had been especially active in its finances, serving for a time as the treasurer for its Youth organization. He also became a member of the PSI's central committee, where he took credit for helping to bring De Michealis' close friend, Benito Craxi, to power as head of the party-- and Prime Minister. He also arranged for ENI to help finance the take over the newspaper Il Globo, so it could support the PSI-- but the deal never worked out. (It went bankrupt).

His dealings with ENI, and association with De Michealis, eventually brought him into contact with his future partner in international finance, Florio Fiorini. When they first met in the late 1970s, Fiorini was the finance director of ENI-- a position he had half for a decade. As such, he was responsible for depositing billions of dollars in ENI funds in off-shore bank accounts. Part of this money, as it later emerged in a Parliamentary investigation, came from off-the-books kickbacks and skims from Saudi Arabia and Libya-- ENI's two major sources of foreign oil-- and the off-shore accounts it went into benefitted PSI and other politicians. In documents that came to light in the ensuing scandal, for example, Fiorini, along with two other top ENI executives, had apparently authorized the transfer of millions of dollars into a numbered account. #63369 in the Union Bank in Switzerland, which in February 1982 was shuttled into the account of PSI politicians, including Prime Minister Benito Craxi, and then wired to an anonymous fiduciary account in Hong Kong. Even if such surreptitious transfers from state-owned enterprises to the coffers of political parties is tacitly accepted in Italy as part of the "system," and no wrong doing was involved, they gave Fiorini, and his associates at ENI, a perspective on Italian politics, which includes the routing of money between numbered accounts in Switzerland and Hong Kong.

In 1982, Parretti came to see Fiorini on an urgent matter. He was in serious financial trouble. his "Diario" newspaper, for which he had pledged Verzotto's former hotels as collateral, were $3 million in debt-- and facing imminent bankruptcy. Moreover, the Syracusa Football team which he headed, seemed to be missing large sums of money. Subsequently, Parretti was arrested on charges of falsifying the team's books and jailed for a week.

He explained to Fiorini that he had a three billion lire saving certificate-- the equivalent of about $3 million-- that had been given to him, through the PSI, by an unnamed businessman but, given his problems, he needed Fiorini's help in cashing it. Fiorini, who had always thought of Parretti as "De Michealis man", took this as, he explained, "a bit of PSI business". Using his formidable financial connections, he sent Parretti to a small Sicilian bank which accepted the certificate and gave him part of the money.

When the bank checked on the certificate, it found that it was a crude forgery. "Three zeros had been added to a certificate", according to Fiorini, changing a $3,000 certificate into a $3 million one. This debacle led to the re-arrest of Parretti in July 1982, this time on charges with bank fraud. Even after he was released, he was under tremendous pressure to reveal who gave him the certificate. He again went to Fiorini, telling him he needed $27,000 to and go to Hong Kong where De Michealis arranged a job for him at Italy's tuna fish plant (which came under his authority as Minister for State Participations). Fiorini provided him with money to get out of the country .

Parretti stayed only briefly at his sinecure in Hong Kong. In 1983, he turned up in Paris. His connections to the PSI apparently still intact, if not strengthened, he became its Secretary in France. As the "French Connection", as he explained it, he acted as liaison with French Socialist businessmen and politicians, on one hand, and their Italian counterparts, on the other. It was a particularly powerful position to be in, especially now that Craxi was Prime Minister.

To aid in this liaison, Parretti set up a shell company, called Interpart in 1984 with the assistance of another PSI financial backer, Lamberto Mazza. It was strategically located in the 999 square mile kingdom of Luxembourg, which provides such corporations maximum secrecy for their transactions. While this shell began with only $20,000 in capital in 1984, at the end of the year, according to corporate statements,, $1 million in cash had been deposited in its account. Three months later, in April 1985, another $4 million materialized. And in December 1986, it received as infusion of $55 million in cash. As this sixty million dollars flowed in, so did Florio Fiorini, who, after buying his own shell company in Switzerland, became a partner and officer of Interpart.

The Luxembourg money first was discreetly channeled into a few select causes sponsored by French Socialist politicians. For example, Parretti, the liaison for the PSI in France, made available $7 million through Interpart subsidiary's, Interpart editions, to buy the French Socialist newspaper, *Le Matin;* and then turned over 48 per cent of the stock in this company to Paul Quiles, who had been the Defense Minister in the Socialist Government. (In 1987, Le Matin, like so many of Parretti's other publishing enterprises, went bust). Parretti also through Interpart established a shell company for one of the Socialist's main financial backer, Max Theret, called MTI, which was then used by Parretti and Fiorini to buy Pathe S.A with financing supplied by the French state-owned Credit Lyonnaise Bank.

The same $60 million pot was also used by Parretti in 1988 to buy his Hollywood empire through a complicated series of transactions in which Parretti's Interpart and Fiorini's Swiss holding company bought 90% of the Melia Group in 1987 for $90 million. After selling the hotels, they used the proceeds to buy a bankrupt Madrid property company called Renta, which became their holding company, and, through its credit line, advanced $90 million to acquire Cannon Films.

But where did Parretti get the $60 million in 1986? Up until that time, most of his businesses in Italy, including his newsletters, football team, consulting company, and hotels wound up bankrupt. He also seemed pressed for cash as late as February 1986 when he was arrested at the Rome Airport on an extortion charge proceeding from a threat he made to a bank to get a mere $20,000. Such desperation over what in Italy is the price of a car suggests that Parretti had no great reserve of cash.

Parretti himself suggested in his interview with me that the money transferred to Luxembourg came from a Panamian holding company he controlled, also called Interpart, which, if anything, raises the question of where the money in Panama came from. Nor are Interpart's scant corporate records of any use in this regard. His own accountant described the Luxembourg "headquarters" as an "empty room", administered on paper by his wife and daughter. And his independent auditing at the time of the injections, Arthur Anderson, noted its concern that there were not any documents explaining the origin of money deposited in Interpart.

Florio Fiorini offered to answer this $60 million question.

He arranged by fax to meet me on a hot Saturday in July at precisely 4 p.m. in Monte Carlo at "his bank," the Seychelles Island bank. It turned out to be a dog-eared three room suite on a sub-ground level floor of a large apartment building with a travel poster of a palm tree on a beach in the Seychelles Islands plastered on one wall. He was a large, chubby man, with a cherubic face, who, in his safari jacket, reminded me of the character played by Robert Morley in the film "Beat The Devil. "It seemed like an appropriate name for this bank," Fiorini chuckled with disarming honesty, "since it is a shell company". (One of his associates in this "bank", he later mention, is Giovanni Mario Ricci, an Italian financier closely involved with the government of the Seychelles) .

He told me, with a nothing-to-hide angelic smile that he had recently come back from Tripoli in Libya (not Liberia). He explained that he went to Libya on a regular basis because he was a financial adviser to Qaddafi's Libyan-Arab Bank, and had indeed acted as an intermediary in buying and selling assets for Qaddafi. He explained he was in a rush because he was leaving the next day for an extensive vacation on a private island in the Bahamas but he wanted to talk to me about Parretti.

Just two days before, a warrant had been issued in Spain for the arrest of Parretti on the charge that he had been smuggling currency to Andorra. Fiorini seemed embarrassed by this development and eager to distance himself from Parretti. Pointing to a chart of his own holding company, which had six rows of neat boxes in it, he circled the one that contained the Melia-Renta-Cannon-Pathe entity, and said "This is only a small part of our operation.". As he began telling me of his relationship with Parretti, he took out a pad of graph paper, and neatly outlined the story, as if he was writing out a confession.

He explained that Parretti had become "infatuated by the movie media", as he put it. Instead of quietly disposing of the film business, he had hire Alan Ladd, announced new productions at a press conference in Cannes, and became part of the Hollywood scene. He suggested that the secret that lay behind Parretti was the Italian Socialist party, the PSI.

In 1984 when cash first began coming into Parretti's account, Parretti was the representative of PSI. Fiorini explain, "The PSI was the principal, Parretti, its collection agent in Hong Kong." He collected money for the PSI's Youth Organization, published "Diario" newsletters that supported the PSI, worked as a go-between for the PSI and the Italy's state-owned oil giant, ENI. He also ran travel camps for PSI workers, and worked closely with Gianni De Michealis, whose faction prevailed in the PSI. In addition, he collected money for PSI's allies in France.

He then used the political party funds he controlled, and the influence they engendered in banks, to finance his failed attempt to take over Hollywood. If he had succeeded, Italian politicians might have been able to add their highly-informed insights to Hollywood's Godfather-type movies and TV series. Instead Parretti, still cooking lavish pasta feasts, retired to hometown of Orvieto.

THE LAST DAYS OF THE VIDEO STORE

In 1997, mogul Sumner Redstone warned Hollywood
studios that the video store business "is going into the toilet" if it didn't get some help. His company, Viacom, not only owned Paramount, but Blockbuster Entertainment. Rentals from Blockbuster's 6,000 stores put $3.9 billion dollars in the six major studios' pockets, and he argued that "the studios can't live without a video rental business. We are your profit." As a result, the studios agreed to share the cost of stocking

Blockbuster's stores in return for a share of its rental revenues. He won that battle but lost the war. Fourteen years later, two thirds of America's video stores have closed and Blockbuster has gone bust. In April 2011, Dish Network bought it out of a bankruptcy auction with plans to convert what remains of its rental store business to streaming a la Netflix and movie vending machines. The other major rental store, Movie Gallery, had liquidated its 4,700 stores in April 2010.

"The store model is now dead," a former top executive close to Blockbusters wrote me recently. "The move to $1-per-day rentals has done it in."

The pioneer in dispensing $1 rental DVDs out of kiosks in fast-food restaurants and supermarkets is Redbox. It was created in 2004 as a joint venture between McDonald's and Coinstar, which then bought out McDonald's. By doing away with clerks, real estate leases, and the store itself, Redbox created a business model with which no brick-and-mortar stores could compete.

Redbox did have a stumbling block: It had to finance the purchases of new titles weekly. To get the wholesale price of $15–$18 per title from the two main wholesalers, VPD and Ingram, it needed a large minimum order. "The capital needed to fill the . . . machines was outstripping Redbox's earnings," said one person involved in the business. The irony here is the studios provided Redbox a solution. To please an angry Walmart, the studios' largest DVD customer—which sold most of its new titles in the first two weeks of their release—it needed to delay Redbox's releases. So Warner Bros. and Fox made a deal in which Redbox delayed its rentals for 28 days, in return getting the revenue sharing that Redstone had gotten for Blockbuster a decade earlier.

Redbox got its titles at a lower manufacturing price and didn't need to raise capital for large advance payments. Even splitting the rental revenue with the studios, it worked out to no more than it had previously paid wholesalers. Redbox resumed its explosive growth in 2009–2010. This became the tipping point.

The other nail in the video store coffin came from Netflix. In October 2008, it added free streaming of movies and TV series to its $8.99 mail-in service. Content was sub-licensed from Starz at a bargain price. Brick-and mortar stores couldn't compete with $1-a-day rentals and free streaming.

Even with video stores dying, the studios did not lose entirely. While they made about 50 percent less from $1-a-day revenue sharing, Redbox and Netflix, along with Walmart, became their biggest customers. A slim-downed cash cow is better than none.

In 2010, for example, Time Warner harvested nearly $4 billion from its home video unit (i.e., DVDs and Blu-ray), which, though about 30 percent less than the peak in 2007, was still a rich lode. Other major studios did almost as well. The losers included indie and lower-budget movies. Redbox concentrated on the wide-opening Hollywood films that have been hyped with $30–$50 million ad campaigns. Since there is limited space in vending machines, indie movies are often not carried

ᐧ The decline of DVDs accelerated as Netflix moved in 2009 from physical DVDs to streaming movies.

Netflix has tiptoed into the breech. It helped finance one new original series and the 5th, 6th, and 7th seasons of *Mad Men* For the creative community gathered around indie films, the death of the video store presented nothing short of a disaster.

SACRIFICING THE THEATRES

On March 31, 2011,Warner Bros., Sony, Universal, and Fox confirmed their plan to carve a new video-on-demand window out of the theatrical window. It will be called "Home Premiere," and for $30 a movie a couch potato can get a current movie beamed into his home from a DirecTV satellite or over a Comcast Cable just eight weeks after it opens in the multiplexes. This means the home audience can see a movie in high-definition in the comfort of their home at least three months before it is available at Netflix, the vending machines of Red Box, or at the video stores.

To these four studios, this is a new window of opportunity. The math, at first glance, looks appealing. The average ticket price in 2010 was $7.89. The studio's share is between 40 to 50 percent depending on its deal with the theaters. (Under some contracts, the studio's cut decreases after two weeks.) This means that at best studios wind up with $3.95 per ticket sold. But for every Home Premiere viewing they wind up with $21 (after giving DirecTV and Comcast their cut.) Even if people watch it in groups, studios can afford to kill off five ticket sales at the box-office per home viewing, and still make money. According to the estimate of a Warner Bros. executive familiar with the research, the studios expect this service will skim off no more than 5 percent of the theater audience. As the Warner Bros. executive calculated it, "we cannot help but make money."

The studios hoped not only to harvest money from this new service but also to draw away part of the growing Netflix streaming audience. The downside was that it put the multiplexes on the sacrificial altar. The economics of the theater business is fairly precarious. Virtually every modern theater is in a leased premise, with theaters fixed overhead, and a payroll to meet. It makes most of its money, not from the proceeds of movie tickets, but from popcorn and ad sales. The concessions have an 80 percent profit margin; advertising, 90 percent. Together, these two operations, which studios do not get a penny from, provide 75 percent of the multiplexes operating income. If they lose only a small fraction of their audience, this income diminishes accordingly. So how seriously would a 5 percent drop in attendance hurt them? A former senior studio executive who was also responsible for that studio's movie theater investments, pointed out that in 2000–2002 just a 3–5 percent drop in tickets sold caused almost half of all the theaters in the US to file for bankruptcy. He added ominously that "A 10 percent drop in ticket sales, and the attendant decline in concessions income and advertising income will close over two-thirds of the American movie theaters—and they will never re-open."

If so, the studios, which now are run mainly by former TV executives, are undertaking a highly risky business. They are offering the public the possibility of watching new movies at home without the hassle and expense of hiring a baby-sitter, driving to a megaplex, and buying food at the concession stand. True, such an offer may appeal to only a small part of the theater-going audience, but their assumption that it will not hurt theaters is nothing more than "I-can-have-my-popcorn-and-eat it too" wishful thinking.   As Hollywood and streamers move   entertainment moves into the homes, the theatrical experience will be sacrificed.

DOWNLOADING FOR DOLLARS

Up until 2007, the studio's principal access to the home market came through pay-tv, free television, video rentals, and DVD sales. But now, with products such as Apple's iPod and TiVo-type digital recorders becoming widely available, Hollywood is continuing its relentless pursuit of the couch potato.

Disney's ABC network, for example, deal in 2010 with Apple will allow iTunes users to download and watch shows for $1.99 an episode. The other networks, CBS, and NBC, a subsidiary of NBC Universal, are selling their programs for 99 cents a viewing via linkups with cable and satellite providers.

This downloading strategy is particularly appealing to the broadcast networks because, unlike cable networks, broadcast networks presently get little cash compensation from cable operators. (Though this is changing as broadcast stations negotiate retransmission fees from cable and satellite operators.) But by offering their hit programs for downloading the next day, networks get cash from the cable audience. A cost of 99 cents a pop is hardly trivial when multiplied by a cable audience of thirty or so million. The downside is that they may lose part of their regular TV viewers, and the advertising revenue that goes with their loyalty. But the networks are betting that their regular audience, which can watch the programs free, would have little incentive to wait a day and download them for a fee.

The studios stand to gain even more from a huge audience willing to pay to download movies from their libraries. Unlike DVDs or Blu-rays, which require manufacturing, warehousing, distribution, and disposing of returns, it costs almost nothing to download a movie or cartoon. Indeed, all of the costs of transmission would be borne by the cable operator (or a site like the Apple iTunes Store), whose cut would be less, under present arrangements, than retailers get on DVDs. So if a movie were a huge hit, such as *Shrek*, and millions of orders flooded in, the marginal cost of filling them would be near zero. The consumer, once he bought the download, could watch it where and when he chose to, just as he once watched a DVD.

The real issue for the Hollywood studios is how they can dig into this potential gold mine without undermining their existing revenue streams.

With the possibility of costlessly providing millions of downloads to consumers of both their older and new films, the studio heads, including Disney's Robert Iger, are openly discussing a radical revamping of the window system. Obviously, if a home download of a movie were available at the same time (and price) as its DVD release, the download option might replace retail sales. To avoid that outcome, and a potentially dangerous confrontation with Wal-Mart, the studios would have to delay the download release until well after the DVD release. But while the studios may find this embarrassment of choices somewhat paralyzing at present, as more and more consumers get digital recorders or video iPods, downloading for dollars may prove short-sighted. The Internet is a place in which films can be streamed as well as downloaded. What the studios' were prying open in their greed for new platforms was what was to become their own digital coffin.

NETFLIX'S FALL AND RISE

Netflix had been a phenomenal success up until 2011. It began as a mega video store that took orders for DVDs over the Internet and delivered them in red envelopes through the US Post Office. A large part of its appeal was as a huge aggregator of film titles. Because it bought physical copies of almost every DVD title that was released to video stores, it could offer its subscribers any title from any studio soon after it was released. It could rent these DVDs because of the so-called "first sale" doctrine, which says that if you buy an item, you can resell it or rent it, so long as you do not copy it.

Meanwhile, the entire video business was being upended by new technology. By 2010, Redbox, which dispensed DVDs from vending machines, for less than one dollar a night, was undercutting brick-and-mortar stores, who, with their higher rent and overhead, could not compete. The two largest DVD rental chains, Blockbuster and Hollywood Entertainment, entered bankruptcy, effectively killing the studios' system for licensing newer titles on DVD. As these stores closed, consumers, unable to find a nearby source for older titles and television series (since they were not carried by Redbox), turned to Netflix to fill the gap. But even though Netflix's growing numbers impressed Wall Street investors, Reed Hastings, the founder and chairman of Netflix, had to consider the uncertain future of the DVD. The DVD was merely a convenient means of storing a movie. It had been adopted by Hollywood studios in the late 1990s and had replaced VHS video in a few years because its smaller size made it easier to ship. But it was based on twentieth century technology that was developed before it was feasible to stream movies directly to consumers and store them in the so-called cloud. It was only a matter of time before the DVD was replaced by streaming, cloud storage, and other twenty-first century technologies. When that happened, Netflix's postal delivery system would be bypassed.

Hastings therefore decided to build a streaming service. In 2008, he offered Netflix subscribers free streaming of movies to supplement their mail deliveries of DVDs. Copyright law prevented Netflix from streaming the DVDs it purchased. Instead, it had to license the electronic transmission rights to each and every title it elected to stream. Hastings therefore made a four-year sub-licensing deal with the Starz pay-tv channel, paying about $25 million a year. Since these rights had little value in 2008, Starz was happy to add $100 million to its bottom line. This gave Netflix access to a large number of titles for streaming since Starz had output deals with two major studios, Disney and Sony, as well as its own original programming.

By 2011, Streaming proved so immensely popular with Netflix subscribers that Hastings decided to redefine Netflix as a streaming service. His plan, which he announced on his blog, was to spin off the mail-in service into a separate company that would be called Qwikster. What remained would be a digital deliverer that would have no need for red envelopes, postage stamps, shipping centers, disc cleaning, or an inventory of DVDs. To pressure subscribers to move to this digital service, he planned to raise prices for Qwikster. Of course the new Netflix would no longer be the aggregating service on which its success was built. Now its subscribers would receive only the newer studio movies via Starz. The problem here was that the deal with Starz expired in February 2012.

When Starz signed the Netflix contract in 2008, it did not foresee the rapid growth of streaming. By 2011, however, it became clear to Starz executives that Netflix's streaming was competing with its own pay-channel, and, even more importantly, with those of the cable and telecom systems who were Starz's principal clients. These clients were now demanded pricing "parity," which meant it would have to change the terms of the Netflix contract so that it could not undercut the prices of its clients. This change would force Netflix to charge premium prices for these newer films, which would mean abandoning Netflix's policy of charging a single price for all its titles. When Netflix refused to accept this change, Starz broke off the negotiations, and announced in July 2011 that it would not renew the Netflix deal.

Without Starz, Netflix would be without a deal giving it access to the films of two of the largest studios, and, as a result, would not be able to provide any of the newer films from the five largest studios, Warner Bros., Disney, Fox, Sony, and Universal, until eight years after they were released to the video stores. This would reduce Netflix to a niche service for older movies and TV series.

Meanwhile, Netflix subscribers began rebelling at the change. Many refused to join Qwikster to obtain DVDs by mail, and others, unhappy with the selection of movies for streaming, quit Netflix. So Netflix reversed itself and eliminated the scheme. Qwikster was killed and Netflix provided both mail-in and streaming. As a result, it still had all the costs of running the mail-in service as well as the costs of obtaining licenses for its streaming services.

As Netflix's other contracts expire in 2012–2013, its other content suppliers, including television networks, will also hike the price. To stay in the game, Netflix's licensing cost will rise, according to the estimates of content providers, by at least a half billion dollars. That is in addition to the $1.2 billion it is presently paying to license digital content (including its deal with EPIX).

This seeming financial roadblock forced Netflix to take a detour that would change the world of entertainment. It would produce its own content. What choice did it have? While there is a plethora of digital entertainment in the world, there is only a limited number of movies and television series that people will pay to see. This is the premium content that Hollywood establishes in theaters, hypes through $40 million ad campaigns, attaches the names of iconic stars, and, in the case of its TV series, shows on the major television networks. Unless Netflix broke Hollywood's monopoly over premium content, it would be out of business. Since there was no shortage of writers, directors, stars and talent agencies mercenaries willing to sell their talents to make movies and TV series, Netflix broke that monopoly.

TRADING ANALOG DOLLARS FOR DIGITAL PENNIES

In early 2008, a top studio executive, discussing the previous year's revenue numbers, said, "Who in their right mind would swap these analog dollars for digital pennies?" The "analog dollars" he went over with me were indeed impressive. They came from DVDs (though they are not analog products), pay television, cable and network television, local stations, and licensing products. The "digital pennies" he referred to came mainly from downloading from Amazon Video on Demand, the Apple iTunes Store, and other websites. Since most of the audience still watched their movies on TV sets rather than on their computers, he saw little reason for the studios to jettison what in the past ten years had proved to be a highly lucrative business model for a nebulous one. The studios' 2007 numbers powerfully supported his point. The six major studios' "analog dollars" amounted to $42.9 billion, with $8.8 billion coming from theaters, $16.2 billion coming from pay and free television, and $17.9 billion from DVDs. That year, the studios' "digital dollars" from downloads amounted to less than $400 million.

Less than two years later, this same top executive had radically revised his thinking. He said that the home TV sets on which 100 million Americans watched the studios' movies, either on DVDs, pay-tv, or free-TV, would soon act as computers. The "tipping point" will come as new sets allow the audience to surf the web with their remote control. By the end of 2010, almost all major TV manufacturers in Japan, Korea, and China will equip their sets with this technology. At the very minimum, this development will mean that the TV audience will have at their fingertips an immense amount of non-Hollywood product.

Consider that in 2009 alone, YouTube streamed more than 9 billion videos; Hulu, a service that did not even exist in 2007, sent TV programs to 35 million computers, and Microsoft's Xbox, Sony's PlayStation, and other game machines had 40 million users. Clearly, as couch potatoes become web surfers Hollywood will have to compete with all this material for their limited time, or "clock."

Even more threatening, the TV-as-computer hybrid will give the entire home audience far easier access to pirated versions of Hollywood's movies and TV programs.

For most of the twentieth century, Hollywood could control its movies because it had a tangible product: reels of film that it could deliver and retrieve from theaters. But the digital revolution changed everything. Movies now can be distributed by a digital formula. And from those ones and zeroes, the movie can be reconstructed in perfect fidelity by a tiny computer chip. Even with the support of governments, private detective agencies, and armies of litigators, the studios have found it difficult if not impossible to quash the copying of these digitalized formulae over the Internet. Each effort to suppress them has led to more ingenious ways to share them. Consider, for example, the recent spread of "cyber-lockers," which are essentially online storage sites. They hold a large number of movie-sized files that can be downloaded by anyone who has been given, or bought, a password. Because the studios' enforcement agents cannot ascertain the contents of these lockers without the passwords, the lockers are almost impossible to police. Compounding the problem, the hosts are often located in countries outside the purview of American or European copyright laws. As a Warner Bros. technical operations chief explained in 2008, many now serve as "facilitators to access pirated content."

Such piracy cuts directly to the heart of the studios' current practice of staggering the release of their products over a long period—the so-called "windows" system. As Howard Stringer, the chairman of Sony, explained to me, studios depend for their profits on their ability to "optimally leverage" their movies in these different media markets. So after the multiplexes play a movie, it is released first in video stores, then on pay-tv channels such as HBO, Showtime, and Starz, and later on free and cable television. Thus each market gets an exclusive window for its version of the movie. But if the vast home audience can get immediate access via downloads from cyberlockers and other Internet sources, the exclusivity loses its value, and the entire window system cracks. Why should HBO pay $15 million for rights to an exclusive window for the latest Harry Potter movie when its viewers can download it from the Internet?

By 2009, the handwriting was on Hollywood's wall: its windows could not be kept open in an age in which its crown jewels—movies—could be perfectly replicated on a computer. One stopgap would be for Hollywood to attempt to protect its DVD and pay-tv windows by stamping out digital piracy. Such a feat would require not only the cooperation of authorities in every country that could host a website or cyber-locker, but a global campaign to change the values of users who see nothing wrong with sharing digital downloads. Another alternative would be to abandon the windows system and attempt to preempt the effects of digital piracy by releasing movies almost simultaneously to multiplexes, video stores, download services, and television. One top Paramount strategist foresees a scenario in which, after multiplexes are converted to digital projection, "a movie opens on 25,000 screens around the world in a single weekend, and within a week it's available for downloads, Netflix, video stores, and cable television." This would allow the ad campaign—and its word-of-mouth—to promote it in any form that anyone is willing to pay for. Such a drastic remedy could not help but affect which films the movie studios produce, since to activate the interest in a global mass audience, new movies will require universally appealing elements (action, graphic content) and easily comprehended themes.

Hollywood, to be sure, is not a single entity. Between them, the big six studios—Disney, Fox, Time Warner, Viacom, Universal NBC, and Sony—control almost all movie distribution in the

United States. Their corporate parents have very different interests. Universal NBC, for example, makes most of its money from its ownership of television and cable networks, whereas Sony, which owns no television networks, make a large part of its money from manufacturing digital hardware, including its PlayStation, DVD players, and high-definition televisions. These companies also have very different leadership styles. But even if they wanted to collude on their responses to the digital challenges—or on the pricing of downloads and DVDs—they would be prohibited from doing so by both American and European antitrust laws. Perhaps they will fare better than their counterparts in the music business did in suppressing digital copying; if they don't, they will almost certainly suffer a similar withering away of the "analog dollars" that flow in through their staggered windows. The separations between these windows will make less and less sense. It was only matter before studios broke with the status quo and move toward the alternative of simultaneous releases. That point finally came during the pandemic in 2019 when the two largest studios, Disney and Warner Bros, released their new movies simultaneously in theaters and on their streaming services, Disney Plus and HBO Max. With a crash heard around the world, the window system shattered. Hollywood now saw the light in swapping its vaunted analog dollars for digital pennies.

THE DEATH SPIRAL

The movie theater began was at the heart of the invention of Hollywood in the early decades of the twentieth century. Financially, it was the place where every last dime collected from audiences was paid into a "box" in the theater's office which provided the major studios with the money they needed to pay stars and make more movies. Because of the crucial importance of the "box-office," studios found it in their interest to own and control the movie houses. Culturally, the movie house was the place where movie-goers, crowded together in a darkened auditorium to cheer, laugh, gasp, cringe and boo at what they saw on the screen. When synchronized sound was added in the late nineteen-twenties, it so further heightened the theater-going experience that most of the American population made it a habitual routine to go the movies every week. Even in 1929, the year that the Great Depression destroyed jobs and wrought untold misery on America, no fewer than 95 million people a week, or 70 percent of the population, went every week to a theater. They didn't go to see one particular film. They went for a three-hour experience that included newsreels claiming to be the eyes and ears of the world; short slapstick films, such as *The Three Stooges* to laugh at; cliffhanger serials, such as *Flash Gordon* that left them in suspense; a "B" feature, such as a Western, which had happy ending; and finally, the main attraction. The studios didn't need to create this huge audience by national advertising. The new film's title and stars' names on the marquee, the lobby posters, and the movie-clock listings in the local newspapers was sufficient to keep the movie houses full. And the crowded movie house was part of the emotional experience.

Even after the Supreme Court in 1948 forced the major studios to divest themselves of ownership and control of the movie houses, 90 million Americans—more than two-thirds of the population— went to a movie house on average every week bought 4.6 billion tickets. In the next few years, the undoing of this mass audience proceeded not from the change in ownership of the theaters but from the availability of a relatively-new technology, television.

By the early 1950s,almost every American family had a TV set in their home. On it, they could watch sports, singers soap operas movies at no cost and no inconvenience. This competition of free entertainment proved too much for the movie house. By 1958, they had lost over half their audience, selling only 2 billion tickets. It was no for lack of effort. The Hollywood studios tried to counter television with widescreen CinemaScope, immersive Cinerama, multi-speaker surround sound, and epic, three-hour movies, such as *Ben*

Hur, Lawrence of Arabia, and *Dr. Zhivago,* but without success. As it became increasingly clear that Hollywood had lost most of the habitual weekly adult audience to television couch potatoes, the studios sought to create a new one through massive advertising on television. In 2004, for example, they spent on average $30 million per movie buying ads on TV programs in the weeks before their openings. This expensive marketing enterprise succeeded mainly with younger viewers but even that demographic was able to produce a weekend audience of roughly one-tenth of the population. Even though it was a small fraction of the pre-TV herd of movie-goers, it was sufficient, along with the sales of popcorn and soda, to keep the multiplexes in business. The high-cost of turning out this audience, meant a new business model for the studios . In it, they expected to lose money on their average release at the movie houses but, after movies were established at theaters, they would make their profit on the so-called back end, which included video, DVDs, TV and foreign sales.

This model collapsed in 2020. Not only dd the Covid-19 pandemic shut down movie houses, but the movie studios decided to join rather than to fight the phenomena of streaming. By this time, technology in the form of 4K high-definition television sets, 1080 progressive streaming and surround sound speakers, was closing the quality gap between the theater and the home, so there was little loss in streaming movies directly into homes.

By the end of 2020, all the major studios, with the exception of Sony Pictures, had created their own streaming services. The two largest movie studios, Disney (which had acquired the Fox studio) and Warner Bros. together accounted for over half of the nation's box-office. Both not only had their own streaming services but also released their movies on them simultaneously with their release at movie house. While Disney's service, Disney + charged for each movie, HBO Max gave all its movies free to its subscribers. As a result of these simultaneous releases, movie theaters no longer had an exclusive "window" on many major Hollywood movies. As a result, people had less incentive to go to a movie house. The results became evident at the box-office. In 2018, movie theaters had taken in $11.6 billion from ticket sales in the U.S. and Canada whereas in 2021, even after most of the theaters were re-opened they took in only $4.3 billion from ticket sales in the U.S. and Canada. To be sure, there were still a few comic-book based blockbusters, such as Sony Pictures' billion-dollar hit *Spiderman: No Way Home,* but they simply took the audience away from other movies. Overall. movie theaters lost nearly two-thirds of the money their audience in these four years.

With the major movie studios, as well as Netflix and Amazon streaming competing movies to the home audience, the issue for the multiplexes was survival. They had to rebate at least half their ticket sales to the studios—and even more in the case of big action movies such as *Spiderman: No Way Home.* And with the amount they retained, along with popcorn and soda sales, they had to the fixed costs, including rent, for each theater, multiplexes had operated on very thin margins even before the advent of streaming. By 2022, with the studios streaming movies in competition with theaters and pandemic concerns diminishing movie goers, they operated in a sea of red ink. For example, AMC Entertainment, the largest and most efficient owner of multiplexes, lost nearly one-half billion dollars in 2021. Such losses, according to one knowledgeable former Paramount executive, signaled the beginning of a "death spiral" for the multiplexes.

This death spiral would gain momentum as more studios put more of their films on their streaming services. Among other things, such a move was more profitable. Unlike with the movie houses which take around a 50 percent cut, studios kept all the revenue from streaming. Next in the spiral, as people elect to watch movies in the comfort of their home, movie studios will reduce their marketing budgets for the TV ads that help create audiences. In turn, multiplexes will sell fewer tickets. The finale of the death spiral comes when the multiplexes chains wind up not taking in enough money from ticket sales and popcorn sales to pay the rent, the suppliers and the employees. At that point, the multiplexes must either seek bankruptcy protection and close down locations.

Can this death spiral be halted? Just as King Canute had no success in commanding the tide, the multiplex chains have not easy task in stemming the tide of cheaper and more convenient streaming.

EPILOGUE

HELLO STREAMERS, GOODBY STUDIOs

To achieve the seemingly simple objective of getting its movies before the eyes of as many viewers as possible, Hollywood had devised a marvelously complex machine to distribute them. By 2009, this distribution system involved in making tens of thousands of celluloid prints of each major film, having UPS deliver them through regional exchanges on a single days to as many as 16,000 theaters across the country, while at the time spending tens of millions of dollars on TV and radio advertising, to create and drive potential movie goers to each of these theaters, who would collect admissions from those who turned up, and, two months later, remit about half this sum to the distributor. The distribution was even more complex overseas since different versions had to be made for different countries, since bonded agents had to clear the prints through customs, lawyers had to negotiated their paths through local censors and bankers had to do complex currency conversions. Meanwhile, different versions of each film were manufactured into DVDs and videos, stored in warehouses for months, and, when the video window opened, shipped to wholesalers, video stores and vending machine operators. Finally, as cable, Pay-Tv and TV windows opened around the world, which could be years later, still other versions of this film had to be distributed to this licensees. Hollywood executives put up with this convoluted Rube Goldberg-type distribution system not because it was the efficient way but because they got a cut called "rentals" at every stage of the time-consuming process. Put bluntly, it was how the studios made their money. There was an alternative form of distribution that involved none of this complexity. It delivered a movie or TV program in high quality directly in real time, with no intermediary storage or warehousing, to any viewer anywhere in the world with an Internet connection. It was called streaming YouTube,. Netflix, Hulu and Amazon joined the streaming race, and were followed by more than a dozen smaller enterprises. Even as the inevitability of streaming became clear to studios, they still managed to impede it progress through its control of content for a few years. But by 2013, with Netflix using its subscription fees to create its own content, the game was over. Streaming had won.

As the streamers became the major creators of original content, the century-old studios and their distribution arms, withered away, Hollywood's claim on the global imagination with classic films such as *The Godfather, Apocalypse Now* and n, also became a relic of the past. As this money-machine of Hollywood is all but replaced by the streaming economy, , this will be the final edition of the *Hollywood Economist*.

ABOUT THE AUTHOR

Edward Jay Epstein studied government at Cornell and Harvard universities and received a Ph.D. from Harvard in 1973. His master's thesis on the search for political truth (*Inquest: The Warren Commission and the Establishment of Truth*) and his doctoral dissertation on television news (*News from Nowhere*) were both published. He taught political science at MIT and UCLA but decided that writing books was a more educational enterprise. *The Hollywood Economist*, which originated as a column on *Slate*, is his fourteenth book. He lives in New York City.

www.edwardjayepstein.com

Printed in Great Britain
by Amazon

41206838R00165